100 PIANO CLASSICS TO GROW ON

Compiled and edited by
Edward Shanaphy

THE STEINWAY LIBRARY OF PIANO MUSIC

The Steinway Library of Piano Music is published by
Ekay Music Inc., Bedford Hills, New York 10507

Editor-in-chief: Edward Shanaphy
Project Coordinator: Stuart Isacoff
Designed by Luke Daigle/Daigle Interactive LLC
Production by Anita J. Tumminelli

Distributed by Warner Bros. Publications, Inc.
and Ekay Music Inc.

www.musicbooksnow.com

A NOTE ABOUT 'LAY-FLAT' BINDING

This special binding is designed to keep your music book open on the music stand. It will need a slight preparation on your part to help accomplish this. Place the book on a clean, flat surface and open it to a section near the front. With the heel of your hand, apply a gentle but firm pressure at various spots along the spine where the pages meet. Do not strike at the spine, and do not run your hand or thumb along the spine. This could cause the pages to wrinkle. Repeat this pressing process at various places throughout the book to break it in. When you have selected a piece to play, repeat the process again for that piece, and you may also, at this point, fold the book back on itself gently squeezing the binding.

CONTENTS

MUSIC BY TITLE

MUSIC BY COMPOSER

INTRODUCTION

This compilation of one hundred piano pieces is more than a random collection of music for students of the piano. It is at once a source of enjoyable, approachable and very listenable piano music, and an extremely valuable educational tool for teachers and students. Here are the pieces that the masters from the Baroque, Classical and Romantic eras composed for their own students, including those compiled or written by Bach for his young wards, and the very first pieces that Leopold Mozart provided to his son, Wolfgang Amadeus Mozart.

The music in this collection serves as the perfect introduction to the classics for aspiring pianists of any age. They are, in miniature, composed with the same skills and forms that the masters were using on a grander scale for the concert and recital halls of their day. Each piece has been selected as much for its appeal melodically and harmonically as for its educational purpose. The book, in its entirety, becomes a measure of accomplishment within itself since the pieces have been sequenced from early levels of proficiency to intermediate. As one progresses through the book—it is hoped with the guidance of a good teacher—pianistic ability can improve dramatically. This same sequence of proficiency also provides an excellent opportunity for more advanced students and players to hone their sight-reading skills. Please refer to the special instructions included herein for using this book as a sight-reading tool.

Rather than crowding as much music as possible onto a page, as is often the case with large compilations, this collection has been engraved in an enlarged note size and with extended spacing of measures to provide an open, airy appearance, facilitating easier reading and annotating. Each piece has been carefully edited to provide fingerings for playing ease and comfort. An all-inclusive glossary of the musical terms used in this compilation, as well as definitions of titles, is included for easy reference. In addition, the special binding used for this book is designed to keep the music open on your piano. See the special instructions on page vii for the proper use of this binding.

It is our hope that pianists, students and teachers will find this collection to be a perfect source of repertoire to play, whether in recital, for one's own pleasure, or for the enjoyment of friends and family.

– Edward Shanaphy

GLOSSARY OF MUSICAL TERMS

a tempo	return immediately to the previously indicated tempo
accelerando	abbr: *accel.;* gradual increase of temp
ad libitum	abbr: *ad lib.;* tempo has no strict beat; played freely at the performer's discretion
affettuoso	warm; affectionate
allargando	abbr: *allarg.* broadening; spreading: tempo slows, often with an increase in dramatic effect
allegretto	less fast than *allegro* and often lighter in mood
allegro	moderately fast; It.: merry, lively; as a musical term it can mean simply relatively fast and energetic
allegro moderato	less fast than *allegro*
andante	present participle of *andare* (It.): going; also used by non-italians to indicate the fastest of "slow" movements
andante cantabile	*andante* with a lyrical, singing style
andante con moto	added energy to the typical *andante* tempo
andante grazioso	walking gracefully
andantino	a term used by some composers (for instance, Mozart) to mean slower than *andante,* and by others to mean faster
animato	"animated"; past participle of *animare* (It.): to enliven
assai	very; *allegro assai*–very fast; can also be interpreted as fairly fast
cantabile	in a singing style
con moto	with movement; quick; often used in conjunction with another tempo indication such as *allegro con moto*
con grazia	with grace
crescendo	abbr: *cresc.* gradually becoming louder
da capo al fine	an indication to play the piece again from the beginning until the place where the end is indicated as *fine*
DC al fine	see *da capo al fine*
decrescendo	abbr: *decresc.;* see *diminuendo*
diminuendo	abbr: *dim.;* gradually becoming softer
dolce	sweet and softly
espressivo	abbr: *espress., espr.* with expression
fine	the end of the piece
giocoso	jocular; playful: often used in conjunction with another tempo indication such as *allegretto giocoso*
grazia	grace
grazioso	graceful
largo	slowly with great expression
legato	smoothly connected
leggero	light and graceful; also *leggiero, leggermente, leggieramente*

leggiero	see *leggero*
leggiadro	pretty and graceful with slight pressure on the keys
lento	slow
lontano	in the distance; having the effect of sound coming from a distance
ma non troppo	…but not too much
marcato	marked; emphasized
meno	less
moderato	moderate speed
molto	very
mosso	agitated; usually coupled with *meno* (less) or *più* (more)
moto	see *con moto*
pedal simile	continue to pedal succeeding measures in the same manner
pesante	heavily
poco	little; a little bit
poco a poco	little by little
rallentando	abbr: *rall.;* same as *ritardando,* but sometimes implies a relaxation of intensity along with a gradual slowing of pace
ritardando	abbr: *rit., ritard.;* gradual slowing of pace
ritenuto	abbr: *riten.;* unlike *ritardando,* this indicates a more immediate slowing of the tempo
sempre	always, as in *sempre staccato*
senza	without
simile	continue to play succeeding measures in the manner previously indicated
sforzando	abbr: *sfz.;* with a sudden and strong accent
smorzando	abbr: *smorz.* dying away
sostenuto	with a sustained tone; *allegro sostenuto* can also mean sustained at a slightly slower tempo
staccato	notated with a dot, vertical dash or wedge above the note, requiring that the note be played in a detached manner with a slight emphasis, the inverted dash or wedge indicating greater emphasis
stretto	for tempo, usually a hastening of pace, often near the end; in a fugue, for a similar effect of increased intensity, the theme overlapped with restatements of itself
subito	immediately
tempo primo	revert to the opening pace of a piece
tenuto	abbr: *ten.;* sustained, often with a holding back of the meter
tranquillo	in a quiet, tranquil mood
vivace	lively

TITLE DEFINITIONS

Air or Ayre	Usually a piece of a light nature, the term sometimes used synonymously with 'tune' or 'song.' In 16th and 17th century England, they were often songs for the lute.
Allemande	Originally a 16th century German dance in duple meter, it later became an instrumental movement of the Baroque dance suite. In the late 18th century the name was used for quick, waltz-like dances and pieces.
Anglaise	Originally a dance of French ballets in the 17th century, the term was subsequently used for later dances or pieces of English origin or style.
Anna Magdalene	J.S. Bach's second wife. He compiled a famous collection of easy level piano pieces for her.
Aria	Normally a piece for solo voice such as an Air or Song. In the instrumental sense it can imply a melodic piece suitable for variations.
Aylesford Piece	One of a number of pieces composed or reworked by Handel while staying at Lord Aylesford's country estate in England. They were unearthed at an auction of the estate in 1918.
Bagatelle	A short piece, usually for piano.
Bourée	A French 17th century dance usually in quick duple meter with a single upbeat.
Burlesca (Burleske)	A piece in a spirited and jesting style.
Canzonet	Short vocal piece of the 16th century, in a light style of a dance piece.
Capriccio	Composers used this title for piano pieces of a humorous or capricious character.
Charolaise	See La Charolaise.
Choral	A piece set in the style of a vocal ensemble or chorus.
Chorale	A hymn tune of the German Protestant Church.
Contradance	A very popular French dance of the 18th century. Also *Contredanse*.
Ecosaise	In spite of its name, this originates as an English country dance, not Scottish, near the end of the 18th century. Schubert and Beethoven wrote collections of these, all in quick 2/4 meter.
Entrée	March-like pieces often used in theatrical works for entrances of dance groups or important personages.
Fughetta	A short fugue of a simpler style.
Fugue	A contrapuntal piece dominated by a subject which appears successively in all the different voices.
Für Elise	For Elise (nickname of Terese Malfatti, to whom Beethoven proposed marriage in 1809; she turned him down).
Gavotte	A 17th century French dance in moderate duple meter.
Intrada	A march-like piece of the 16th and 17th century.
Invention	Term of obscure origin, used by Bach for his collections of contrapuntal keyboard pieces. Other composers have used the term to title a small piece.
La Charolaise	French for *The Woman of Charolais*.
Ländler	A folkdance of Austria and German Switzerland, usually in slow 3/4 meter.
Les Tambourins	The tambourin is an oblong, narrow drum of Provence, also called *tambour de Basque*. Usually played together with a small flute, the galoubet. The piece in this volume is typical of the flute and drum effect.

Lied	German song.
Lullaby	A quiet piece, usually a cradle song, of lulling character.
Mazurka	A national dance of Poland in triple meter, of moderate speed, most often with a strong third beat; sometimes with an accented second beat.
Minuet	A French dance whose origins are vague. It was introduced to the court of Louis XIV circa 1650 and quickly spread throughout Europe.
Minuetto	Italian spelling of Minuet.
Musette	Rustic dance-like piece that utilizes a held or repeated bass figure (drone) as would have been played on a musette, a French country bagpipe.
Pastorale	A piece that is descriptive of the countryside or that has a rural mood.
Polka	A lively dance in 2/4 meter, originating in Bohemia circa 1830, later in the century becoming a most popular ballroom dance throughout Europe.
Quadrille	Early 19th century French dance, very popular during the Napoleonic era, eventually being replaced by the polka.
Reverie	Dream-like piece.
Rigaudon	A folkdance originating in 17th century southern France, primarily Provence, later becoming very popular in the court of Louis XIV. Like the *bourrée*, it has a lighthearted quality, in four-measure phrases, each with an upbeat.
Rondo	One of the basic forms of classical music, it consists of a series of sections, the first of which is repeated between other secondary sections, and restated for the conclusion.
Roundelay	An Anglicism of *rondeau*, an important form of medieval French music (no connection to the term *rondo*).
Sarabande	A most popular slow instrumental dance of the Baroque era, originating in Latin America and Spain during the 16th century as a sung dance. In triple meter with the stress often on the second beat.
Scherzo	Usually a movement of a larger piece such as a sonata or symphony, in a fast triple meter.
Scherzando	Playful; or playful piece.
Sonatina	An abbreviated type of sonata, easier to execute, and used primarily for instruction purposes.
Tambourins	See *Les Tambourins*.
Trio	Originally a three-voice contrapuntal piece; in a Minuet or Scherzo the Trio is the middle section of the piece coming before the main section is repeated.
Valse	Waltz.
Waltz	The most popular ballroom dance and instrumental form of the 19th century. Always in 3/4 meter, the form reached its zenith with the waltzes of Viennese composer Johann Strauss.
Walzer	Waltz.
Zingarese	Gypsy; a piece in the gypsy style.

SIGHT READING POINTERS

Sight-reading music is a reflex activity that one can develop and improve. However, to do so requires the proper discipline. If a pianist or student finds sight-reading difficult—playing each new piece in fits and starts, fingers cautiously crawling to the next chord, head incessantly bobbing up and down from printed page to keyboard and back again—the experience can be very frustrating, discouraging, and time-consuming. Keep in mind, however, that even some very accomplished pianists do this, and that there is hope for them and for you.

Three essential elements constitute a sight-reading improvement regimen:

Any pianist should begin a sight-reading improvement campaign with folios of simple pieces, baby pieces perhaps, or easy classics in large volumes such as this one. Easy pop books can be helpful as well. Choose the simplest things at first.

The second element is a good metronome. This is the instrument that inflicts the deadline upon your next digital move. It doesn't stop while you find the next note, so setting it at the slowest tempo at which you can negotiate a passage is key. A simple piece might have one or two passages that are slightly more difficult than the rest (just as in any other piece of music). Those are the passages that should dictate your metronome's tempo for the entire piece. Once you have found that tempo, write it lightly in pencil (the third element, a pencil) at the top of the piece.

Later, after you have gone through a series of pieces and your reading is improving, go back and review these pieces at a faster tempo than the one you penciled in. Pencil that new tempo in too, for future reference. As you improve, you'll bring all your pieces up to speed by going back and increasing the metronomic beat, bit by bit.

Helpful hints:

1. Try to think beyond one note at a time. Look at the music in small chunks. Look at a measure, or a chunk, for two seconds; close your eyes; try to remember what you saw. Try to play it. Do this exercise regularly. Again, with simple music. You are training your musical memory power.

2. Play new music slowly enough to be able to look ahead a beat or two.

3. You can sight-read hands separately, the same way you rehearse difficult passages. As you improve, you will find it easier to read both parts at once.

4. Scan a piece thoroughly before you attempt to play it. Look for the difficult spots. Look at the time and key signatures. Tell yourself to *please remember it has two flats*, for example. Start singing the rhythm of the first measures to yourself silently or quietly, before you start playing, to get a feel for the piece. You would be well advised to take a new piece away from the piano and study it in some depth before attempting to play it. You'll be surprised how much better you'll do with this slight preparation.

5. Accent exaggeratedly the first beat of pieces in 3/4 time, and the first and third beats of those in 4/4. This helps keep you in focus, and maintains the pulse of the piece in your mind and hands. It also pushes you along.

6. Try as much as possible to keep from looking at your hands.

7. Don't stop to fix wrong notes. Forge ahead with the inexorable beat of that unforgiving, unrelenting metronome. Let the wrong notes fall where they may; try to pick them up next time around, increasing your batting average of correct notes each time you play a piece through.

8. Limit the sight-reading portion of your practice sessions to ten or fifteen minutes. Don't make it a burden. You are more apt this way to make it a daily and welcome routine.

PIANO CLASSICS TO GROW ON

THE WAYSIDE ROSE

Adolph Köhl

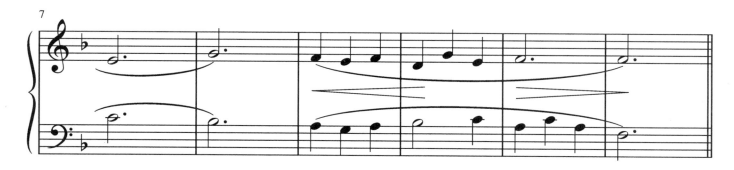

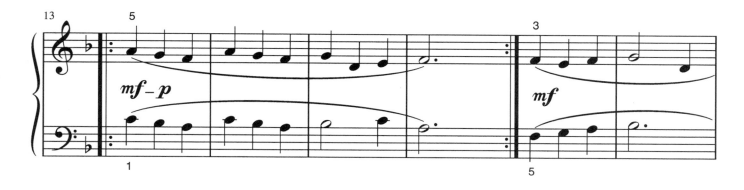

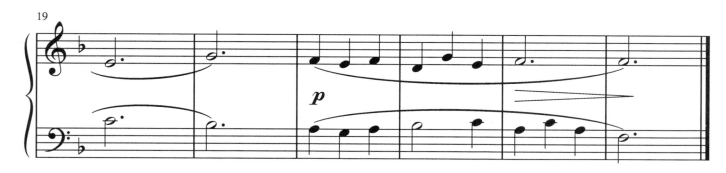

BAGATELLE
in G

Anton Diabelli

CHORALE

from Johann Sebastian Bach's Notebook for Anna Magdalene

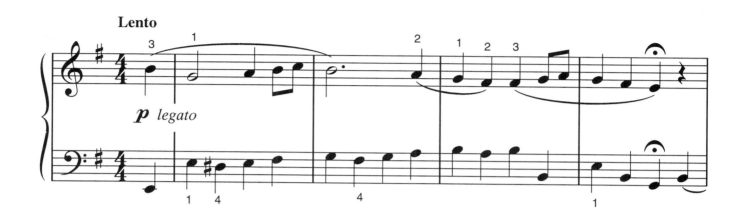

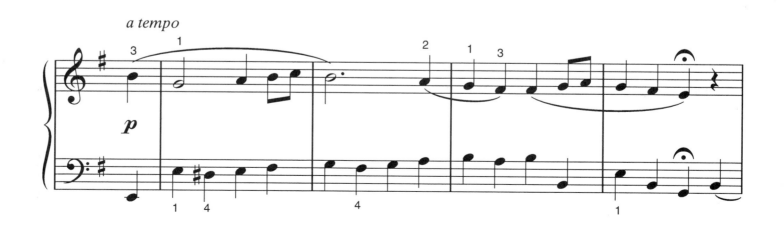

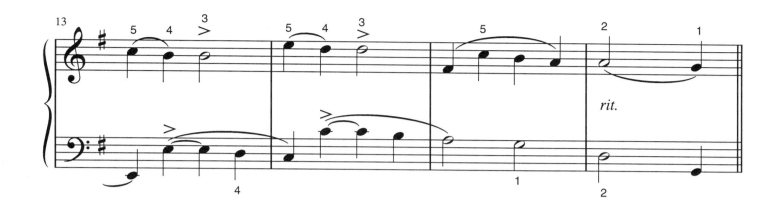

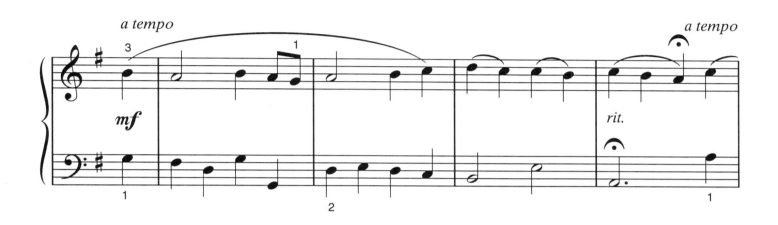

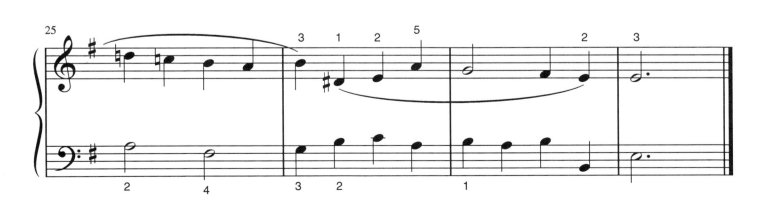

CHORAL

Robert Schumann

LIED
in F

from Johann Sebastian Bach's Notebook for Anna Magdalene

LIED
In D minor

from Johann Sebastian Bach's Notebook for Anna Magdalene

MINUETTO

James Hook

Andantino

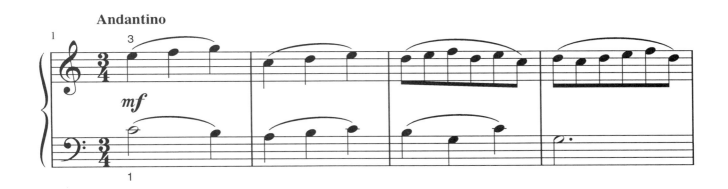

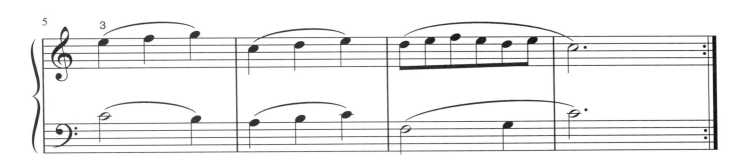

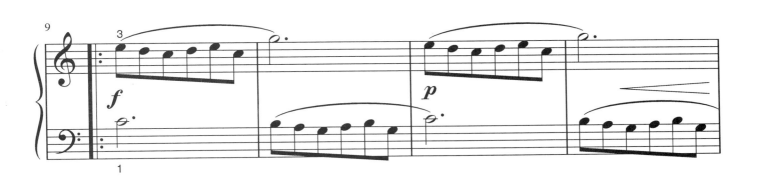

MUSETTE

Felix Le Couppey

CANZONET

Christian Gottlob Neefe

COUNTRY WALTZ

Franz Joseph Haydn

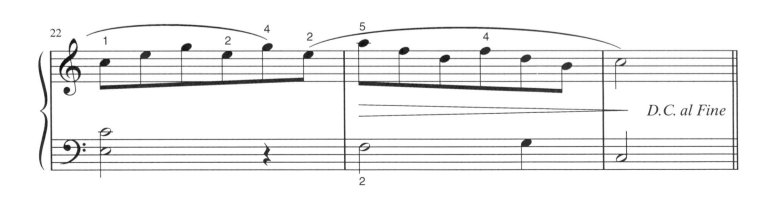

EMPEROR ALEXANDER'S REGIMENTAL MARCH

Ignaz Moscheles

MINUET
in C

Wolfgang Amadeus Mozart

GAVOTTE

George Frideric Handel

Andante

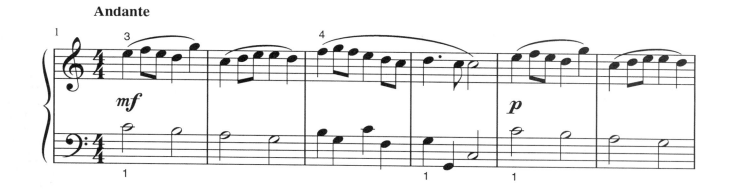

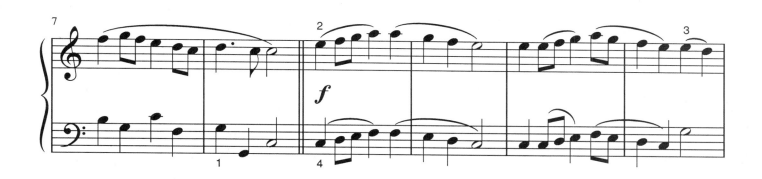

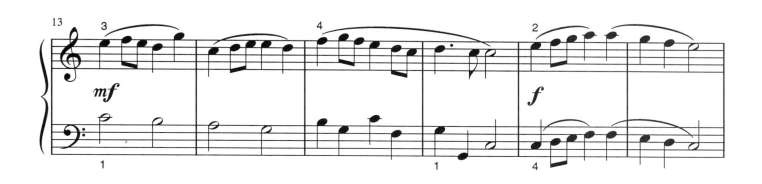

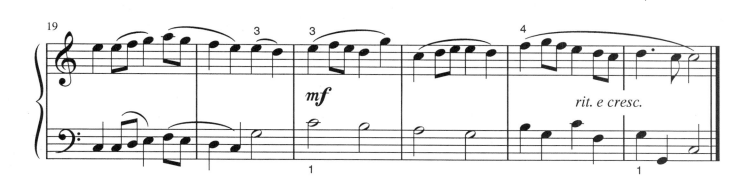

BAGATELLE
in A minor

Ludwig van Beethoven

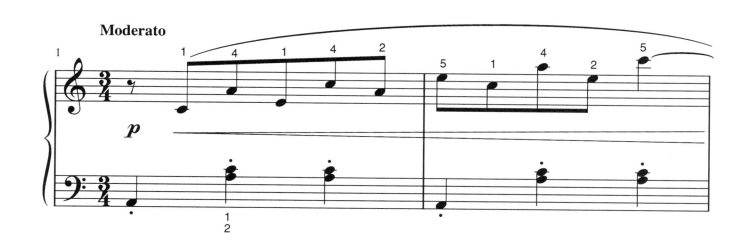

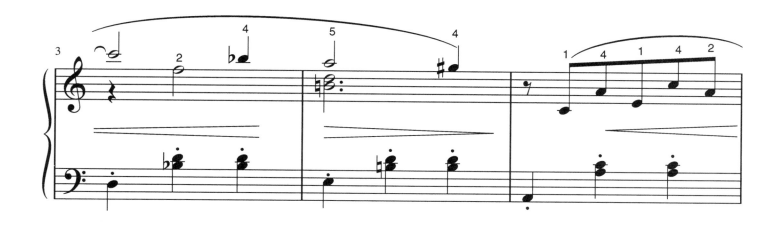

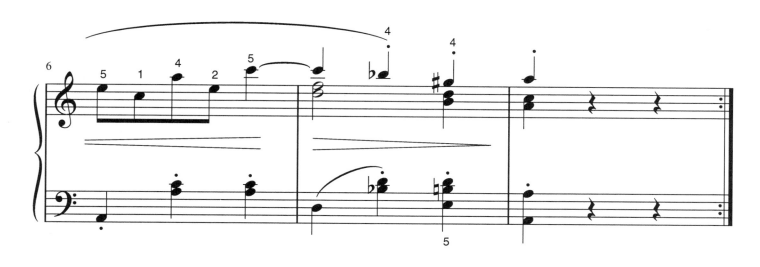

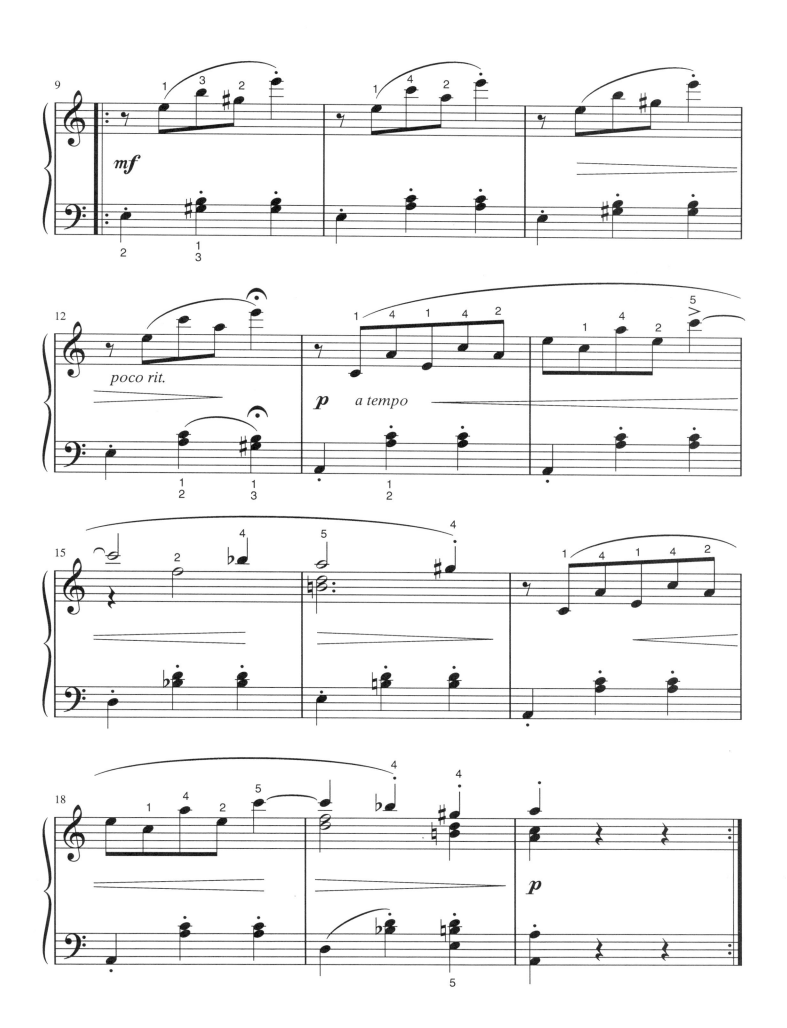

QUADRILLE

Franz Joseph Haydn

RUSSIAN FOLK SONG

Ludwig van Beethoven

LITTLE SUITE
in five-note patterns

Heinrich Wohlfahrt

1.

3.

Allegro

MINUET
in G

from Johann Sebastian Bach's Notebook for Anna Magdalene

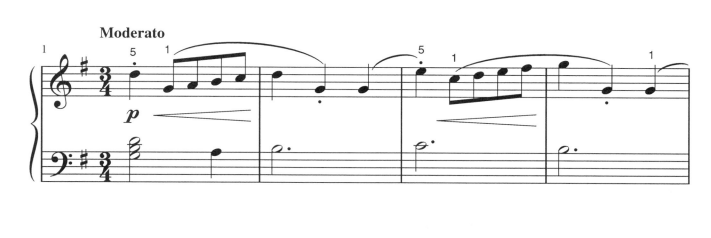

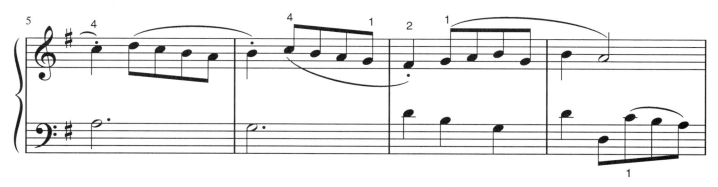

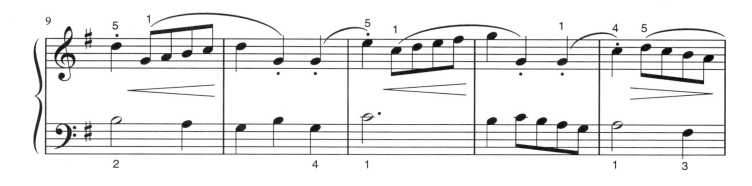

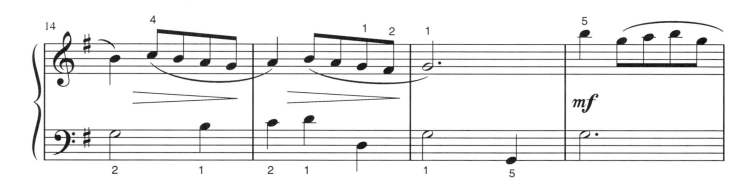

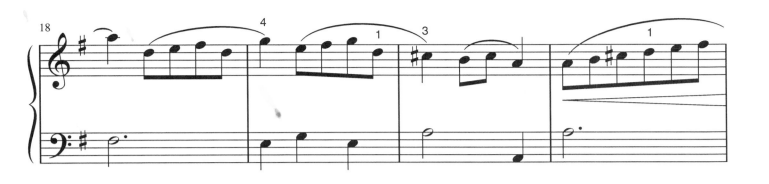

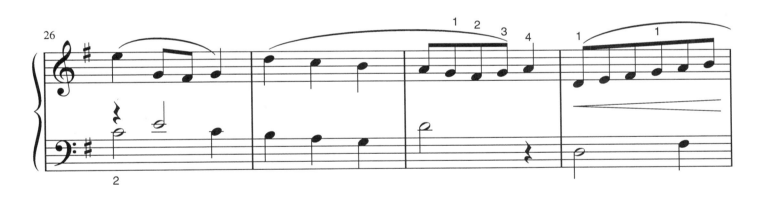

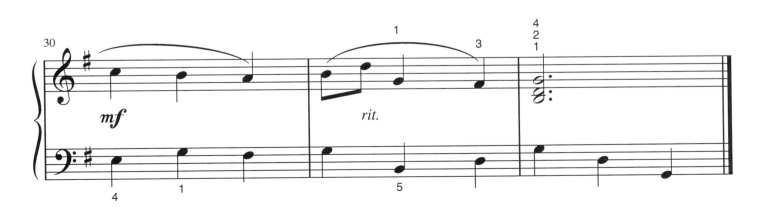

TWO LITTLE INVENTIONS

Jan Jakub Ryba

1.

2.

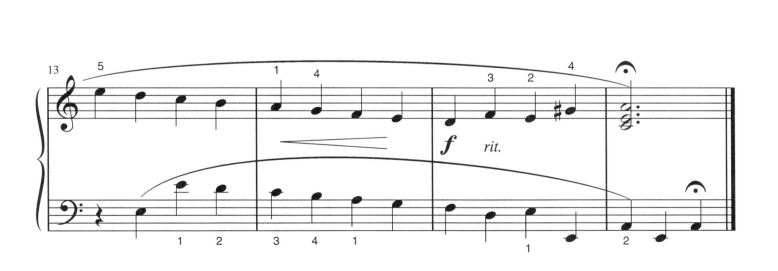

TWO MINUETS

from Leopold Mozart's Notebook for Nannerl

I.

II.

THE SICK DOLL

Pyotr Il'yich Tchaikovsky

TWO AUSTRIAN FOLK TUNES

Louis Kohler

I.

Allegretto

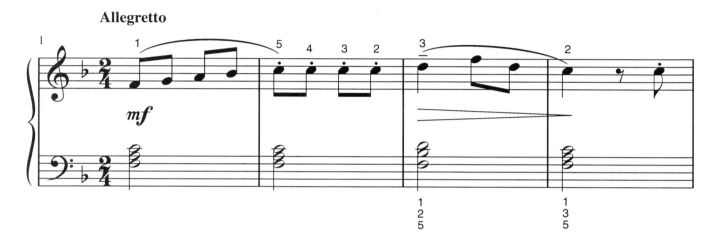

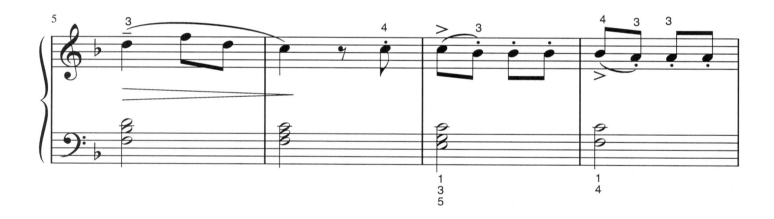

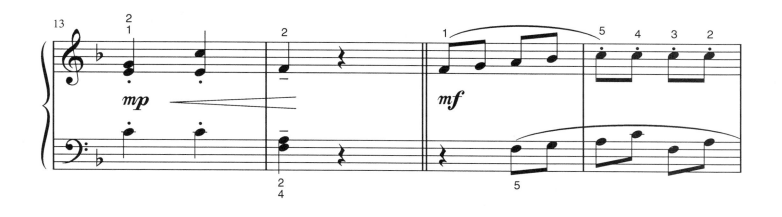

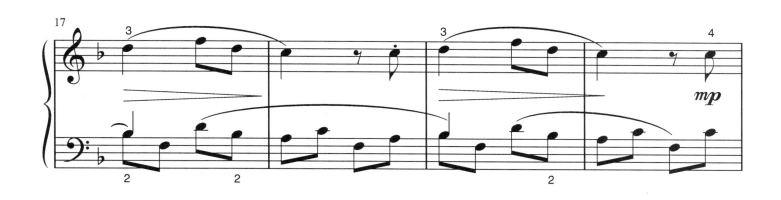

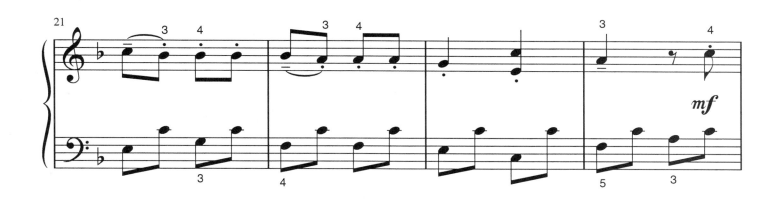

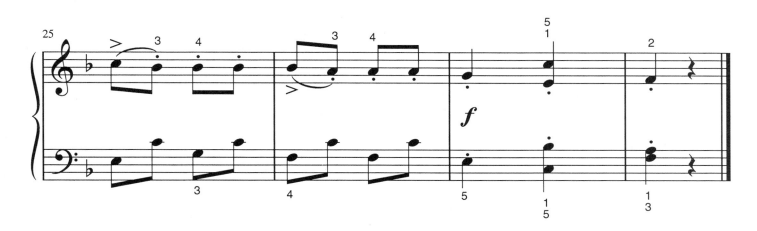

II.

Moderato

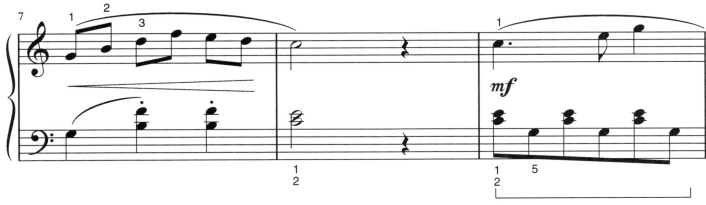

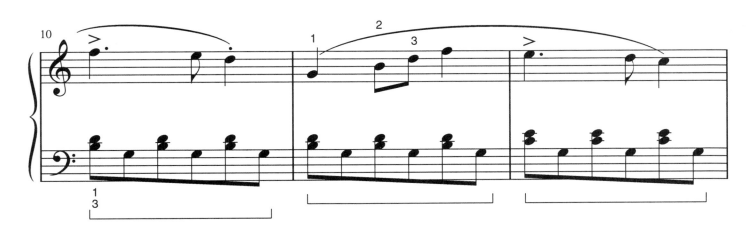

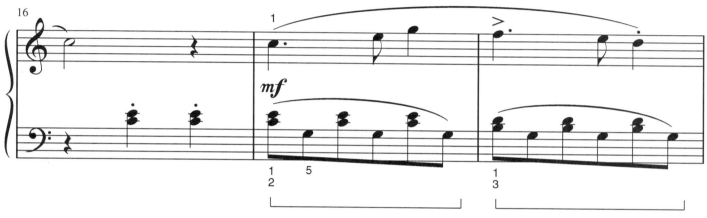

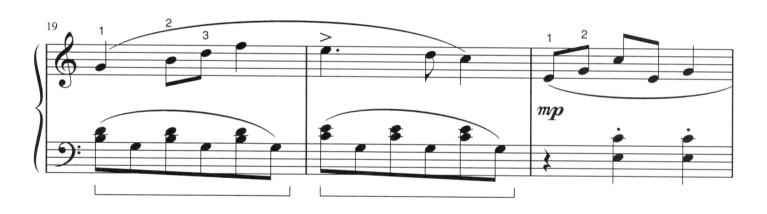

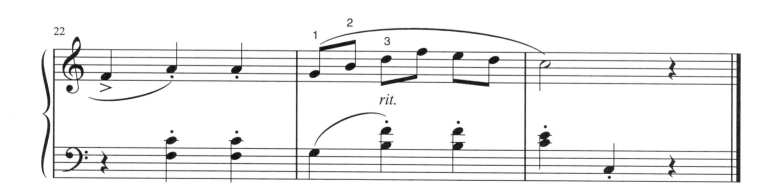

MINUET

Leopold Mozart (from his Notebook for Wolfgang)

TO A WILD ROSE

Edward MacDowell

With simple tenderness (♩ = 88)

ped. simile

(no ped.)

ped. simile

(no ped.)

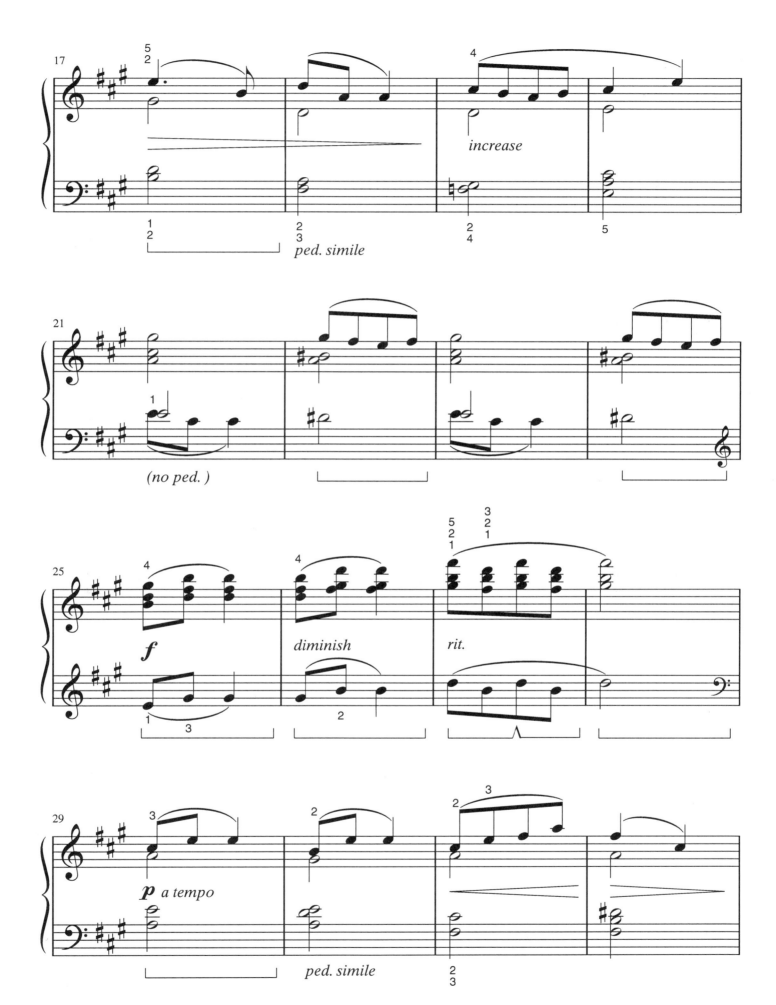

THE ENCHANTED GARDEN

Robert Volkmann

ECOSSAISE

Ludwig van Beethoven

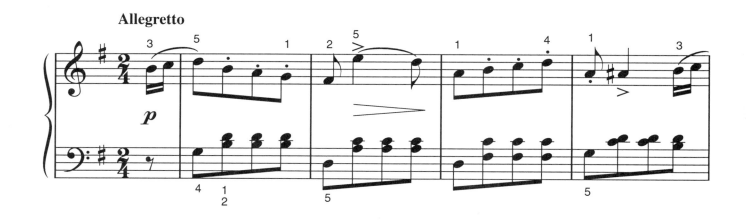

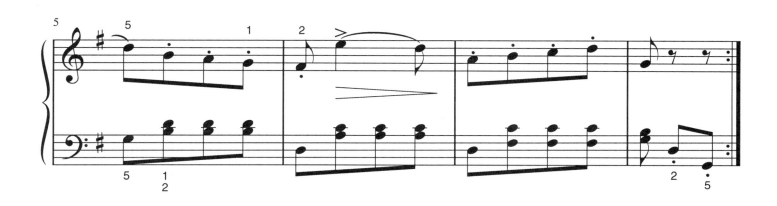

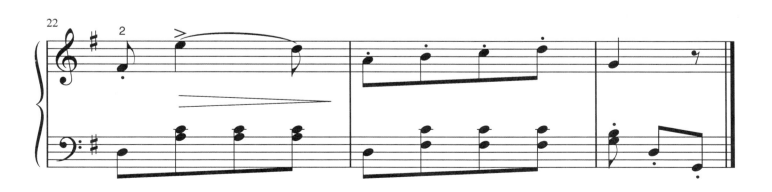

MINUET
in F

Wolfgang Amadeus Mozart

NOËL

Louis-Claude Daquin

MUSETTE

from Johann Sebastian Bach's Notebook for Anna Magdalene

Allegretto giocoso

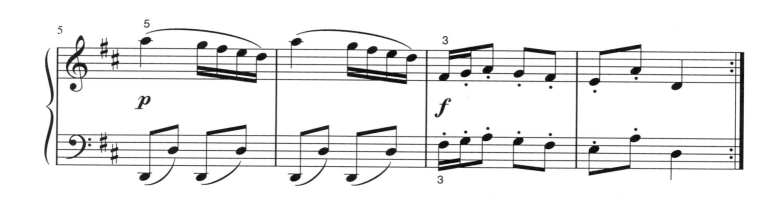

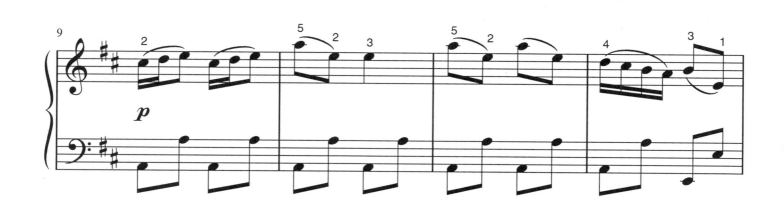

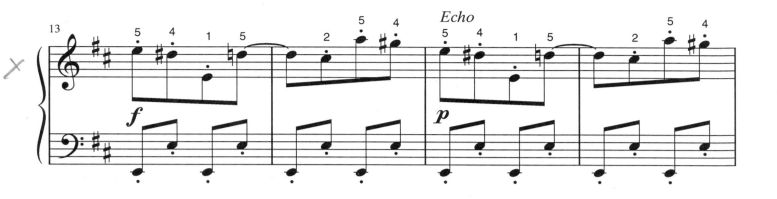

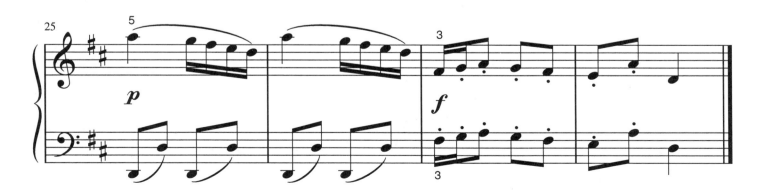

ROUNDELAY

Joachim von der Hofe

ENTRÉE

Leopold Mozart (from his Notebook for Wolfgang)

OLD FRENCH SONG

Pyotr Il'yich Tchaikovsky

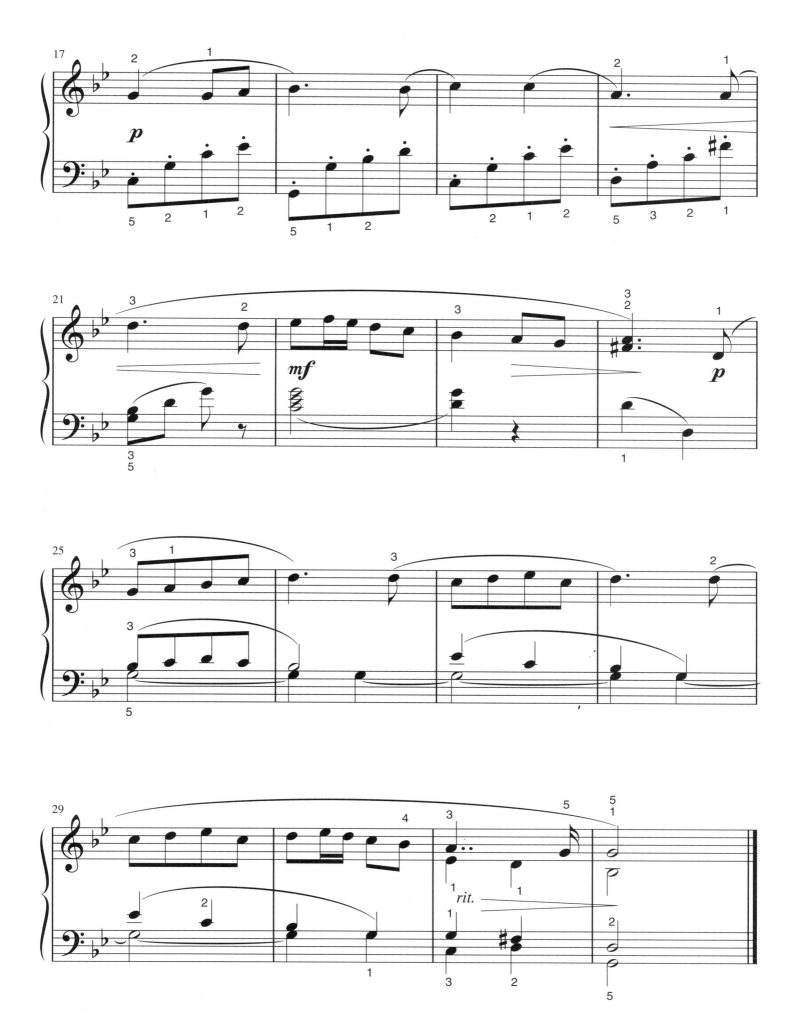

ANDANTE

Anton Diabelli

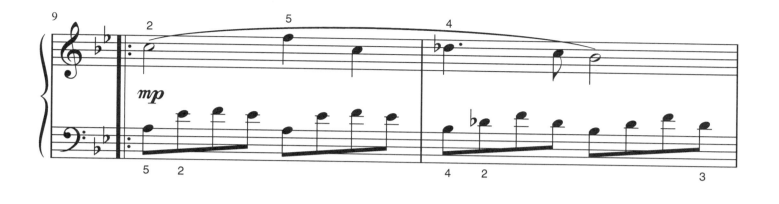

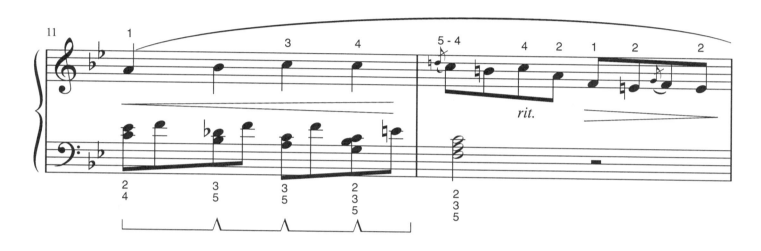

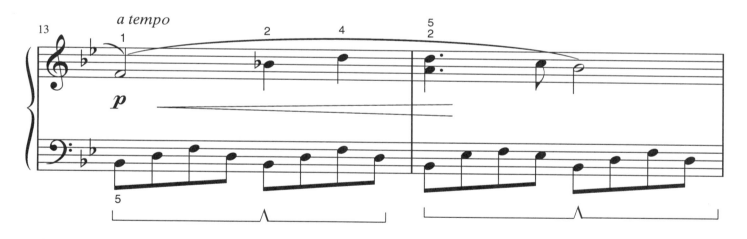

BAGATELLE
in C

Anton Diabelli

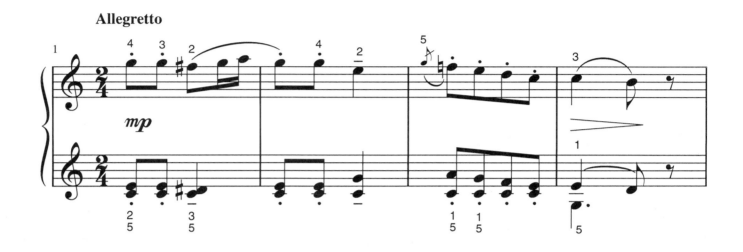

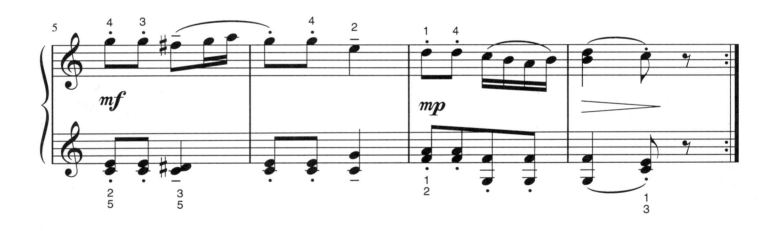

BAGATELLE
in C minor

Ludwig van Beethoven

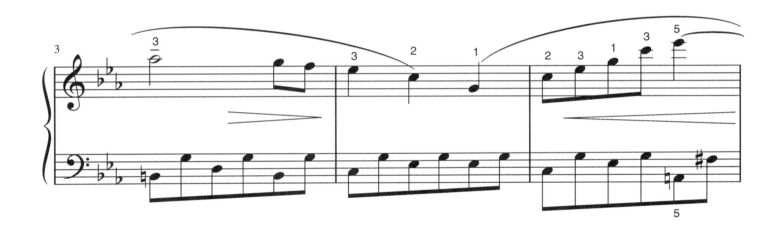

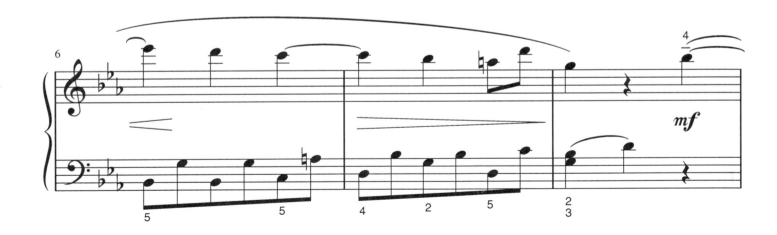

MINUET
in G minor

from Johann Sebastian Bach's Notebook for Anna Magdalene

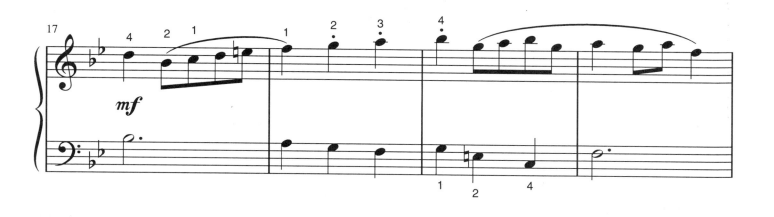

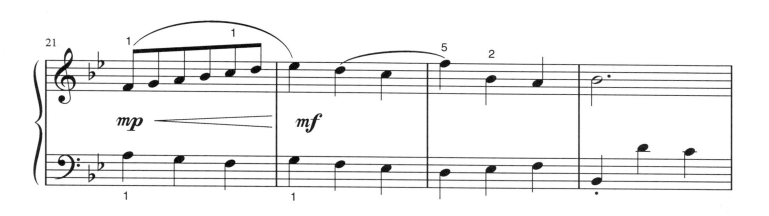

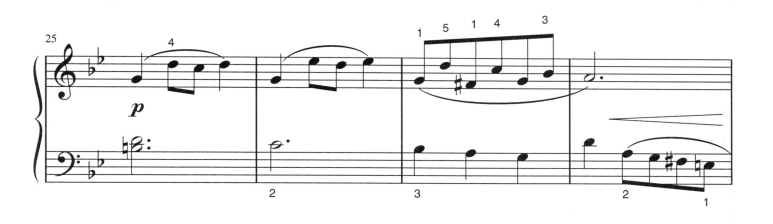

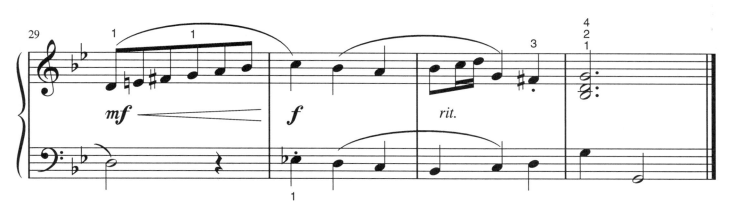

MINUET AND TRIO

Johann Sebastian Bach

Trio

GERMAN DANCE

Franz Joseph Haydn

LA CHAROLAISE

Francois Couperin

SARABANDE

Johann Jakob Froberger

ANDANTINO CON GRAZIA

George Frideric Handel

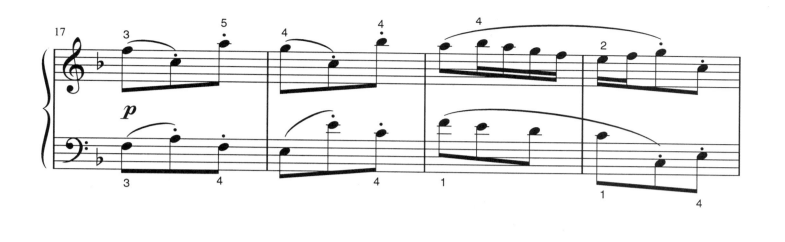

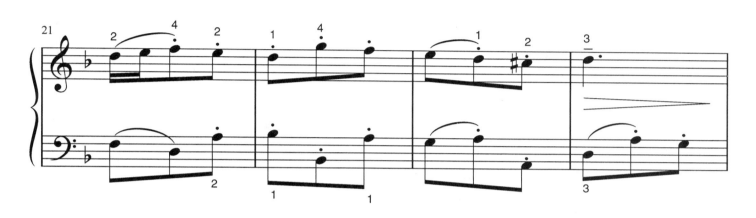

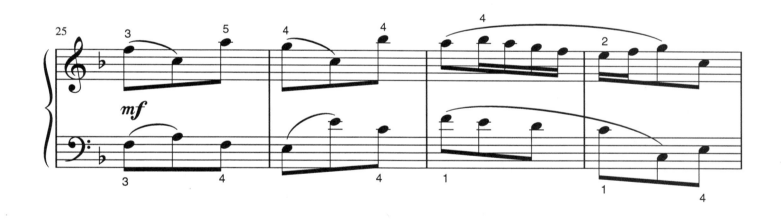

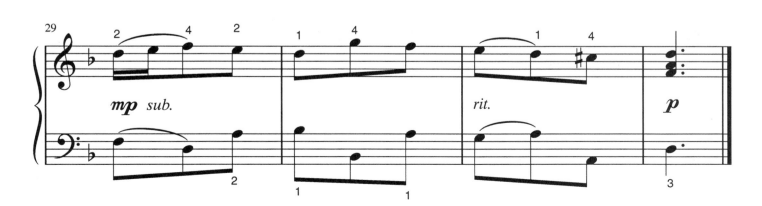

AIR DE DANCE
from Sonatina No. 4

Jean Latour

COUNTRY MINUET ✓

Franz Joseph Haydn

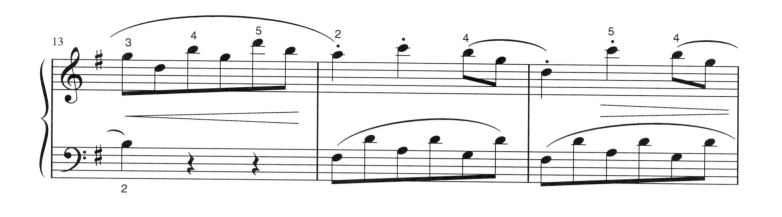

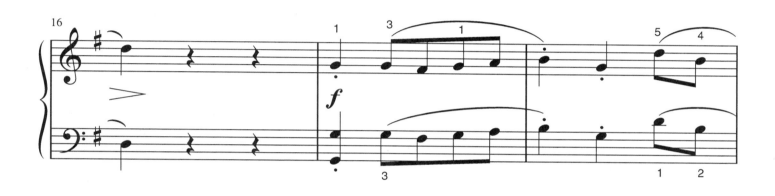

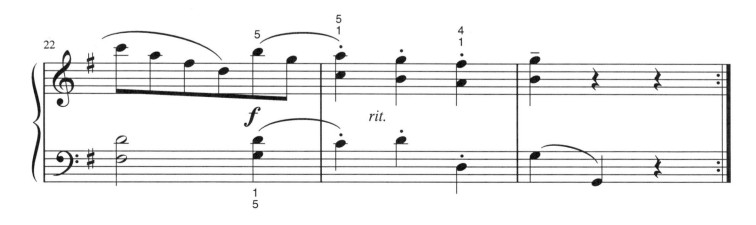

FUGHETTA

Johann Pachelbel

IN CHURCH

Pyotr Il'yich Tchaikovsky

PASTORALE

Friedrich Burgmuller

FIRST LOSS

Robert Schumann

FÜR ELISE

Ludwig van Beethoven

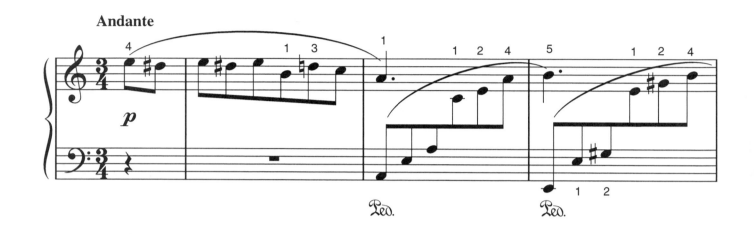

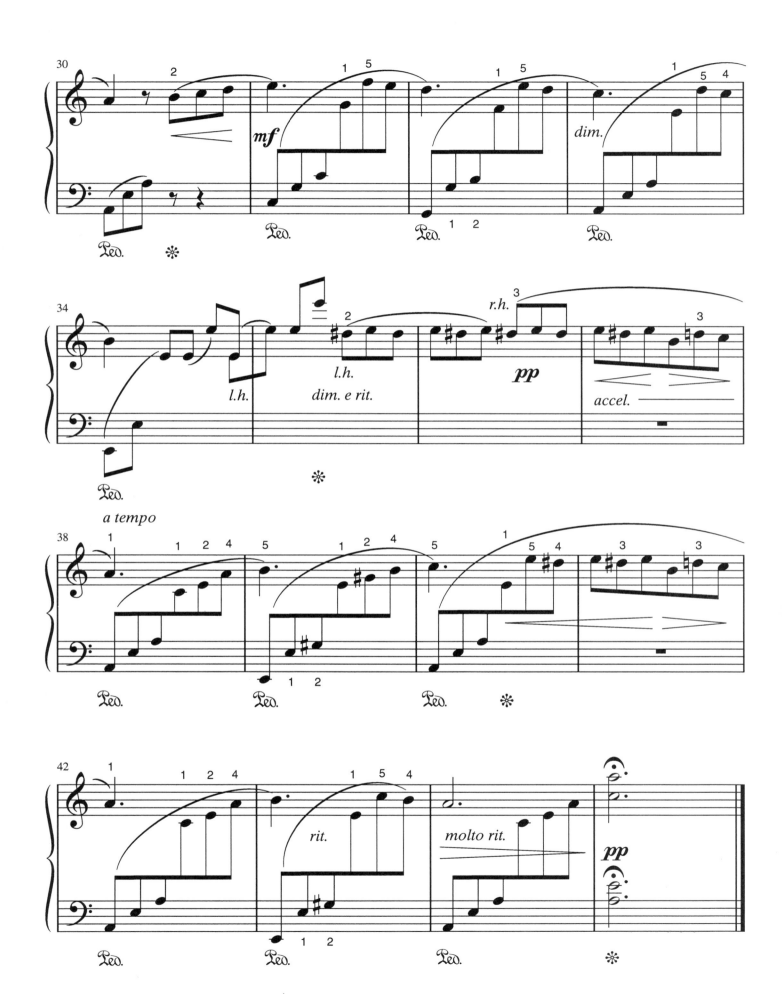

AN OLD ROMANCE

Stephen Heller

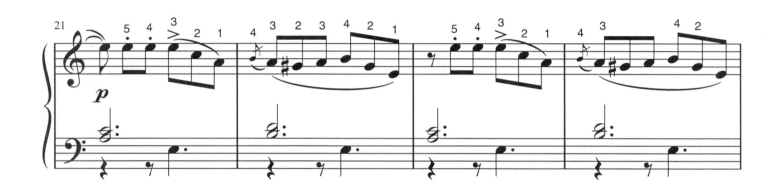

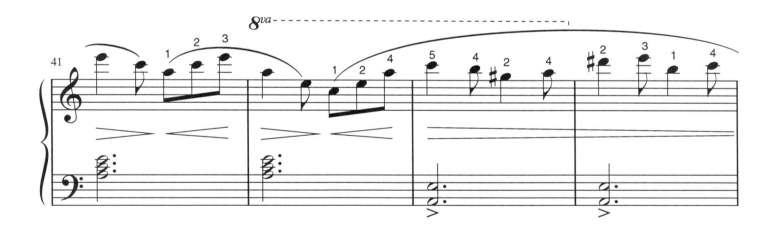

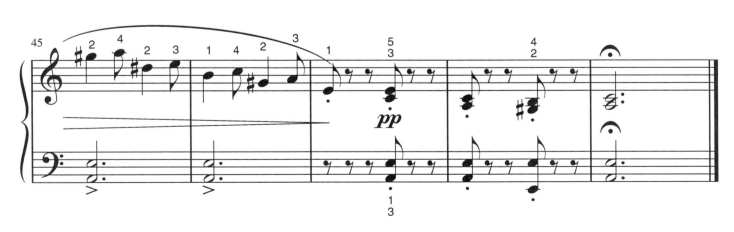

ANGLAISE

Johann Christoph Friedrich Bach

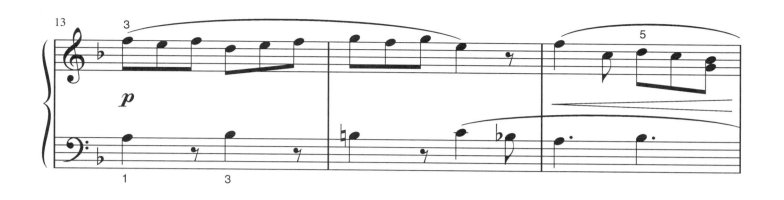

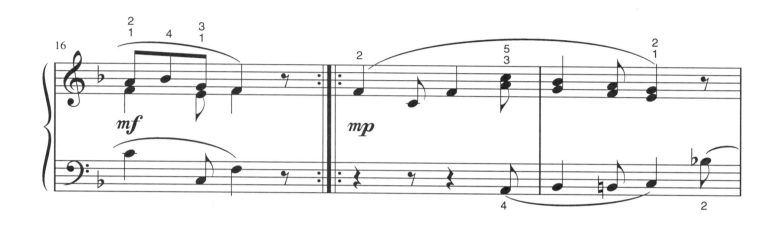

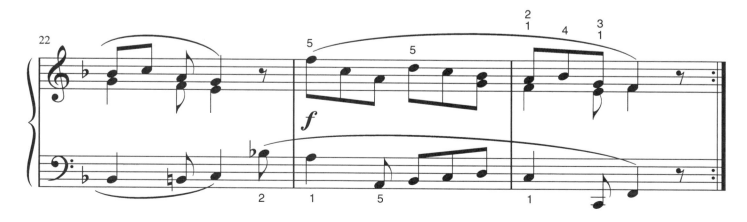

LITTLE STUDY

Robert Schumann

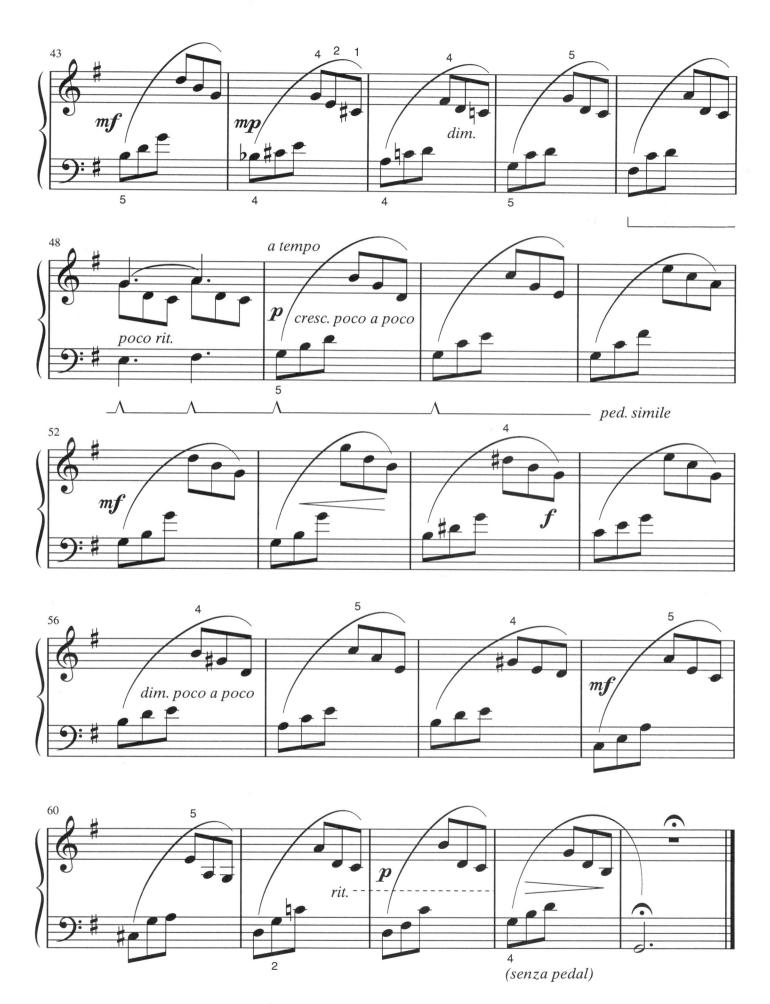

LULLABY

Johann Philipp Kirnberger

ALLEMANDE

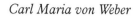

Carl Maria von Weber

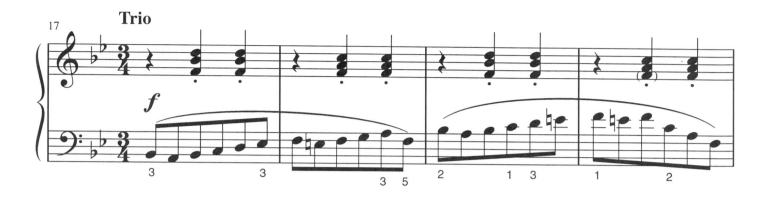

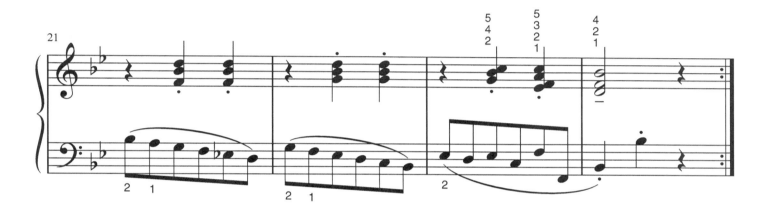

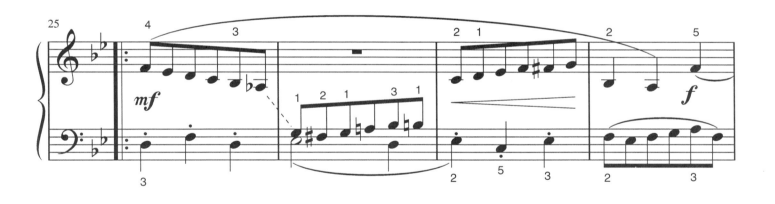

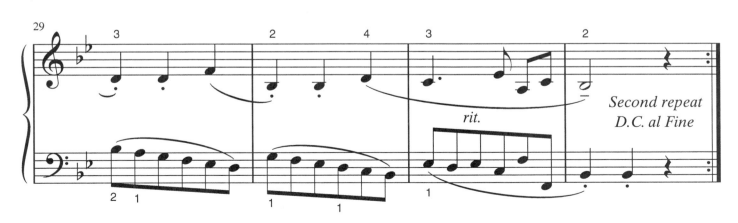

AYLESFORD PIECE

George Frideric Handel

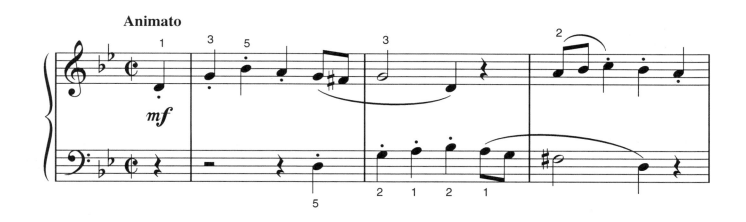

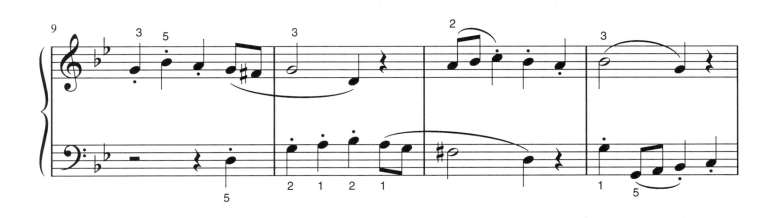

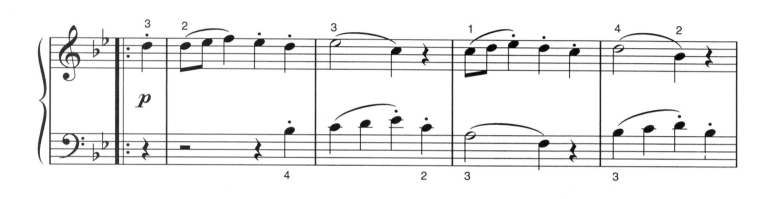

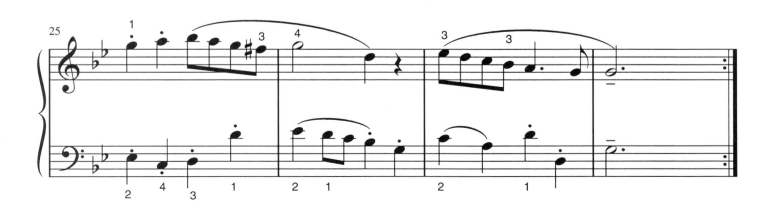

ARIA

George Frideric Handel

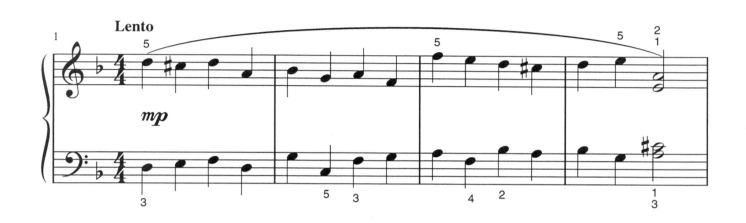

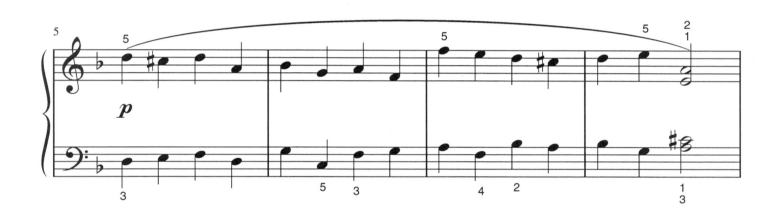

BURLESKE

Leopold Mozart (from his Notebook for Wolfgang)

CONTREDANSE

Heinrich Wohlfahrt

FOLK TUNE SCHERZO

Theodor Kirchner

RIGAUDON

George Frideric Handel

RONDO

Wolfgang Amadeus Mozart

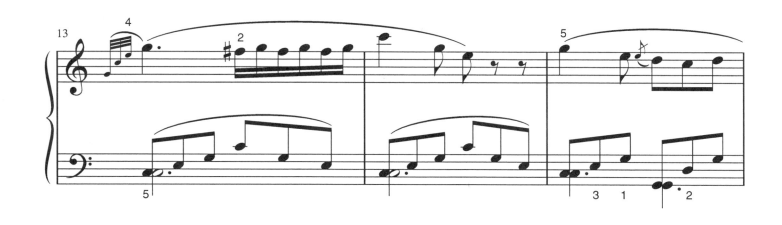

RUSSIAN POLKA

Mikhail Ivanovich Glinka

LÄNDLER

Franz Schubert

TRIO
from Minuet in F

Franz Schubert

MINUET
in G

from Johann Sebastian Bach's Notebook for Anna Magdalene

Moderato grazioso

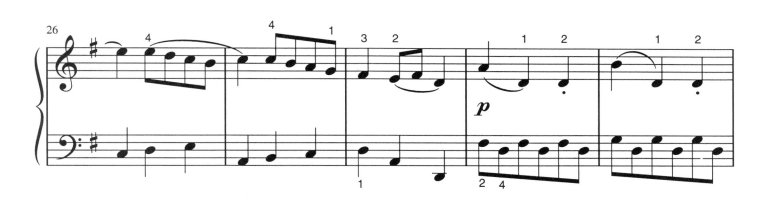

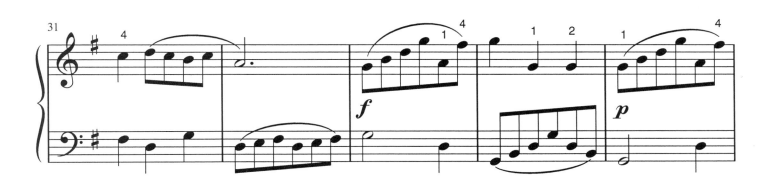

PASTORALE

Carl Philipp Emanuel Bach

BURLESCA

Wilhelm Friedemann Bach

AYRE

Jeremiah Clarke

BOURÉE

Georg Philipp Telemann

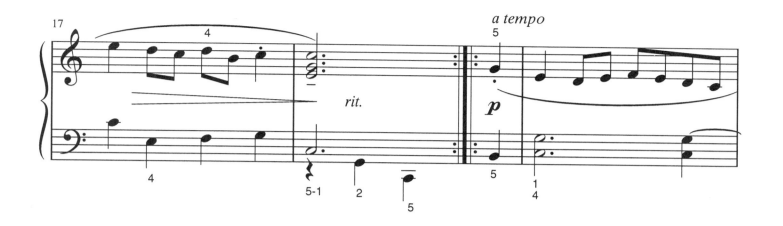

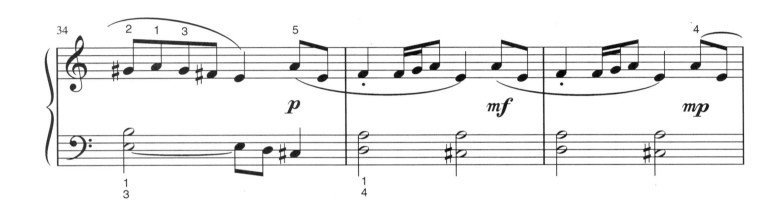

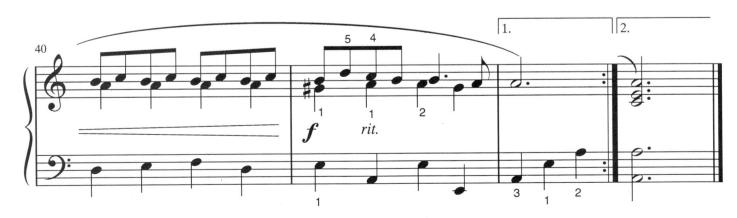

MELODY

Robert Schumann

CAPRICCIO

Johann Wilhelm Hässler

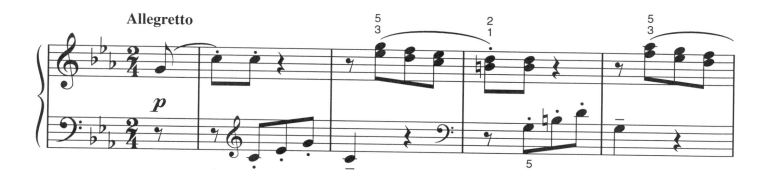

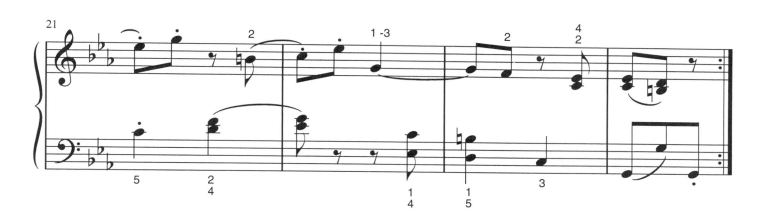

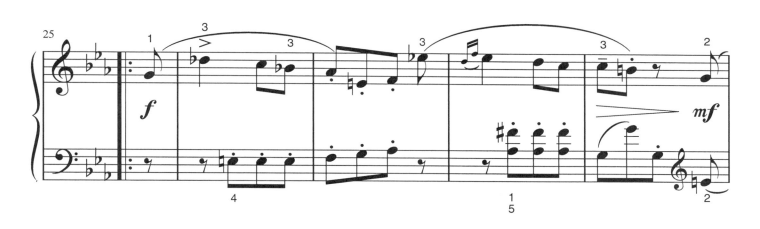

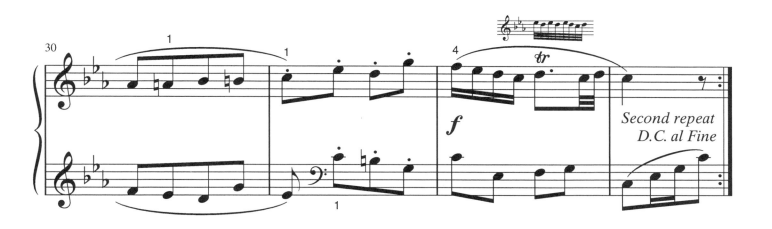

CONTRADANCE
in A

Wolfgang Amadeus Mozart

CONTRADANCE
in G

Wolfgang Amadeus Mozart

ITALIAN SONG

Pyotr Il'yich Tchaikovsky

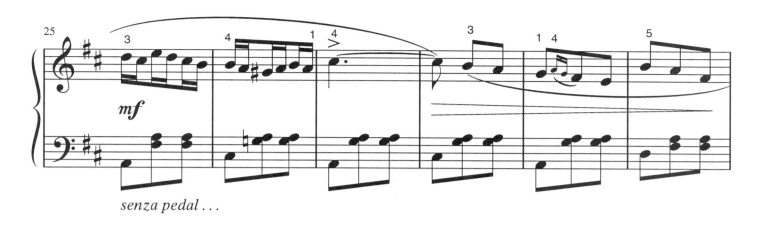

senza pedal . . .

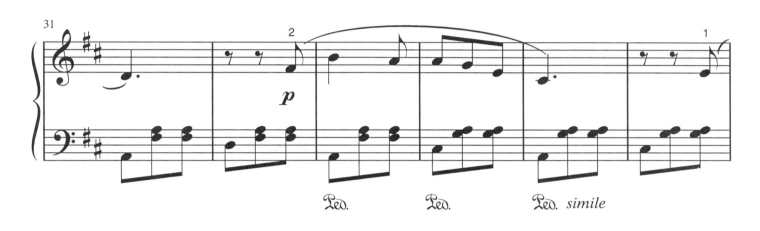

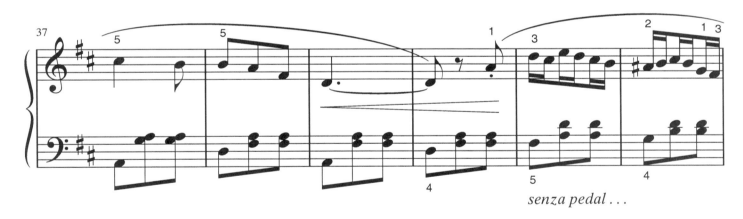

senza pedal . . .

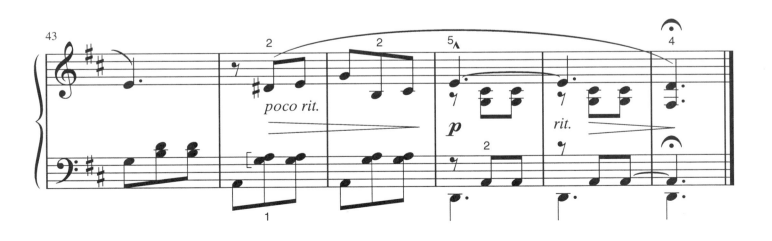

MINUET
in C minor

from Johann Sebastian Bach's Notebook for Anna Magdalene

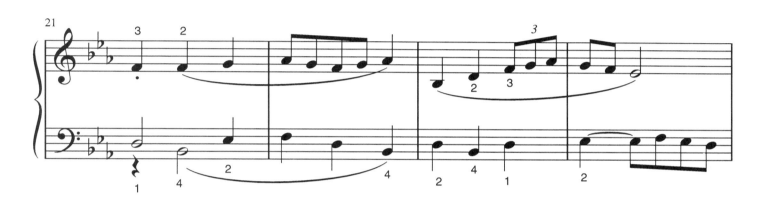

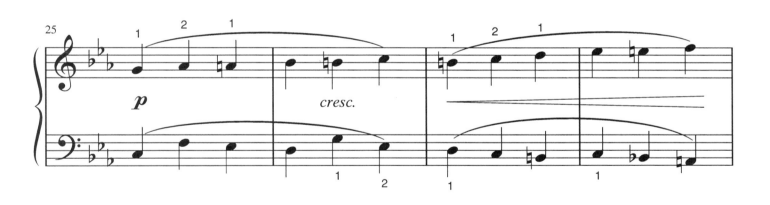

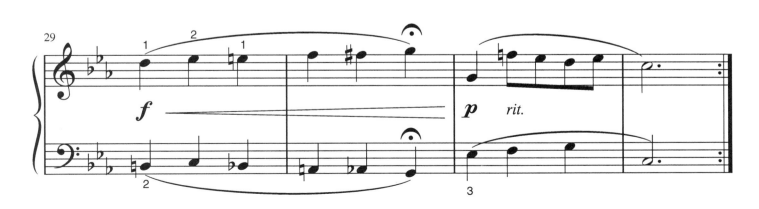

MINUET
in D minor

from Johann Sebastian Bach's Notebook for Anna Magdalene

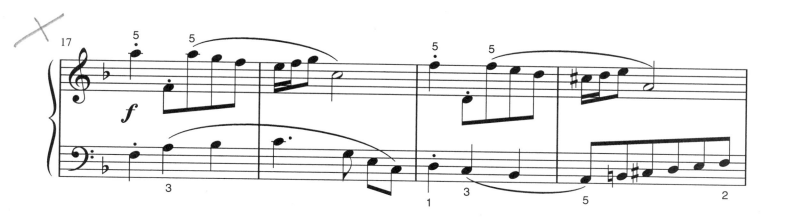

PRELUDE
E Minor, Op. 28, No. 4

Frederic Chopin

REVERIE

Pyotr Il'yich Tchaikovsky

WALZER

Franz Schubert

SARABANDE

George Frideric Handel

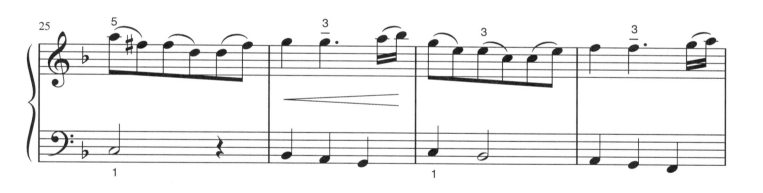

TWO ECOSSAISES

Franz Schubert

I.

Allegretto

II.

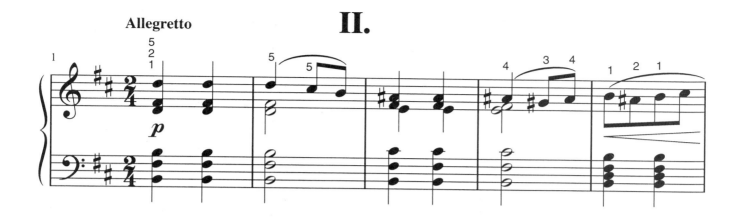

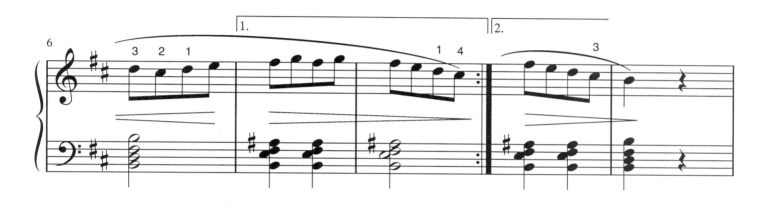

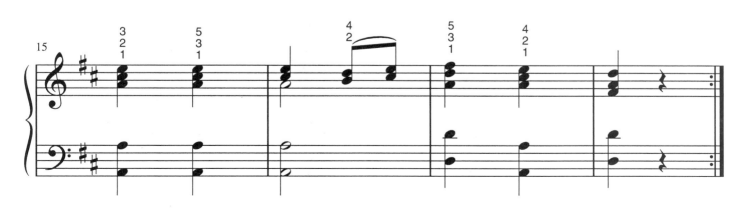

MAZURKA

Pyotr Il'yich Tchaikovsky

Tempo di mazurka

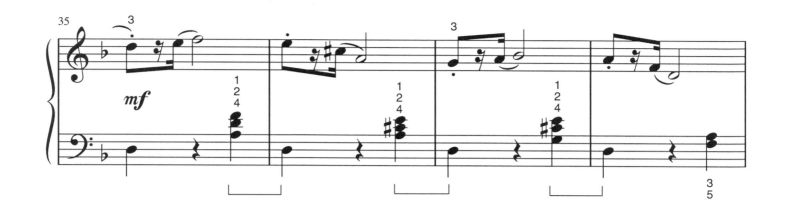

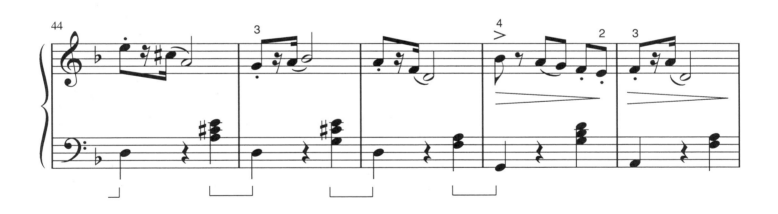

GERMAN DANCE

Franz Schubert

LENTO AFFETTUOSO

Carl Philipp Emanuel Bach

Lento ma non troppo

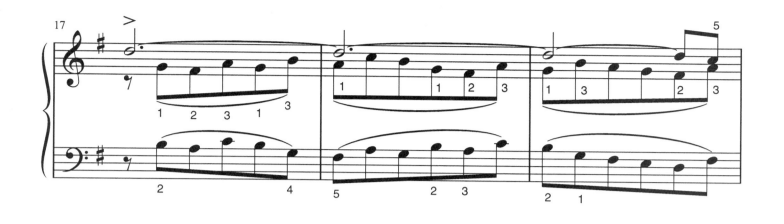

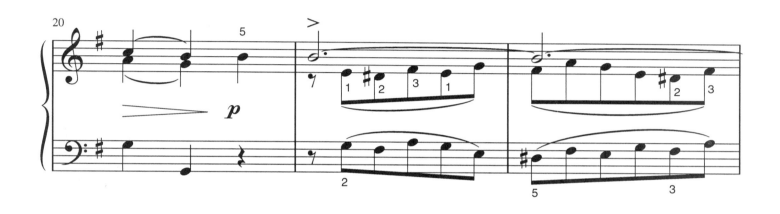

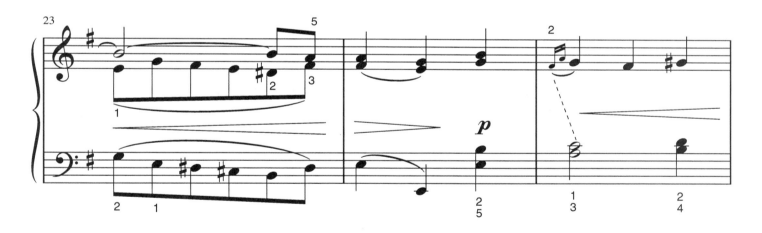

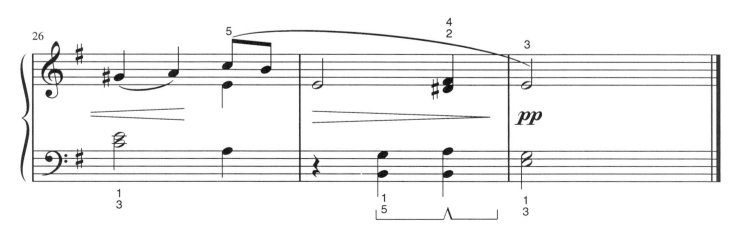

PEASANT SONG

Felix Mendelssohn

Allegro sostenuto

INTRADA

Christoph Graupner

LES TAMBOURINS

Johann Philipp Kirnberger

SPRING SONG
Come, Sweet May

Wolfgang Amadeus Mozart

REAPER'S SONG

Robert Schumann

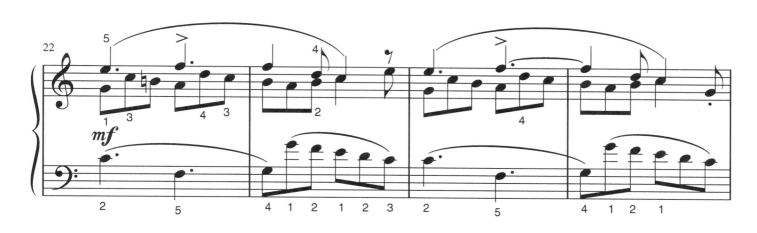

RUSTIC DANCE

James Hook

SIX GERMAN DANCES

Ludwig van Beethoven

I.

II.

III.

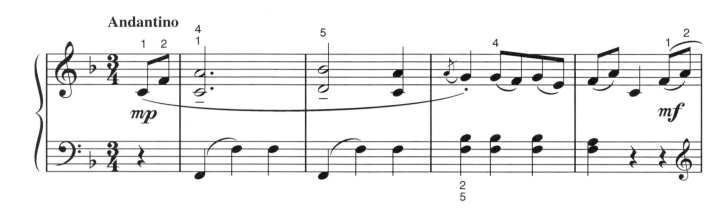

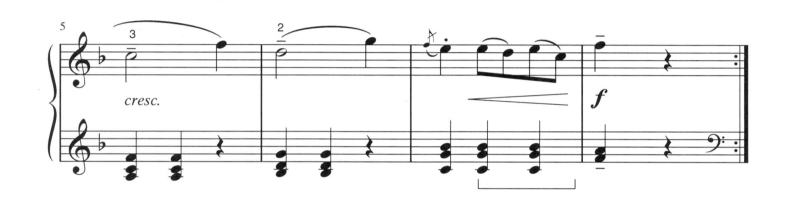

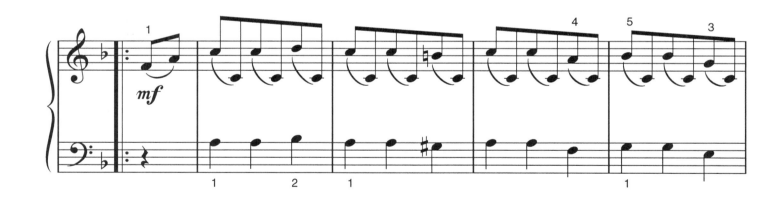

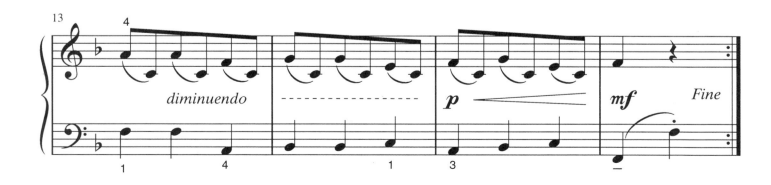

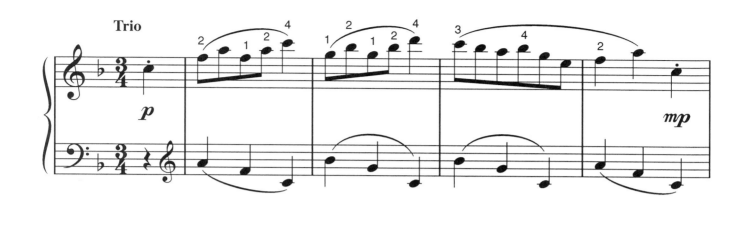

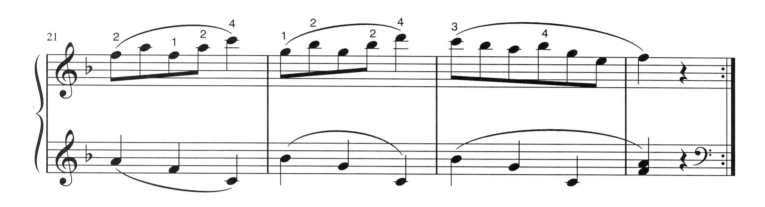

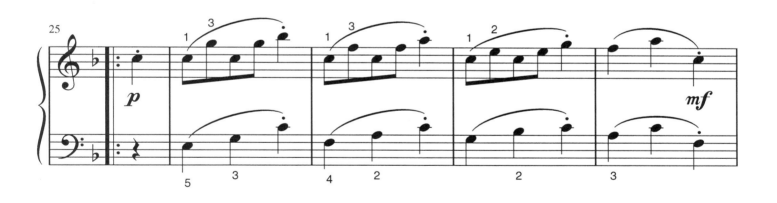

Da capo al fine
2nd time

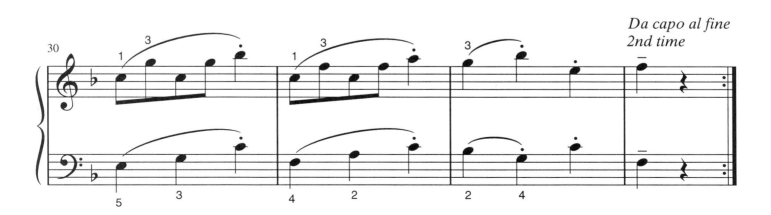

IV.

Allegretto

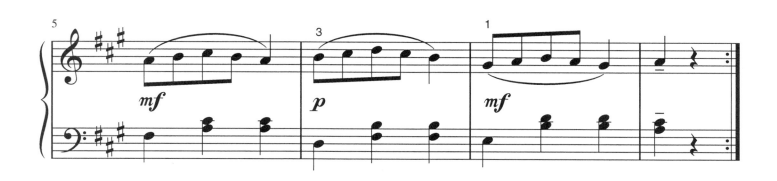

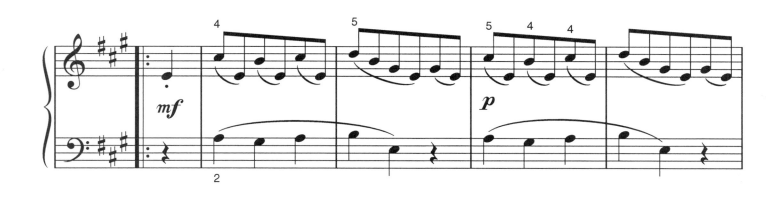

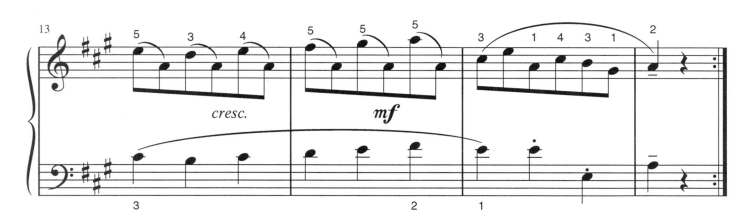

V.

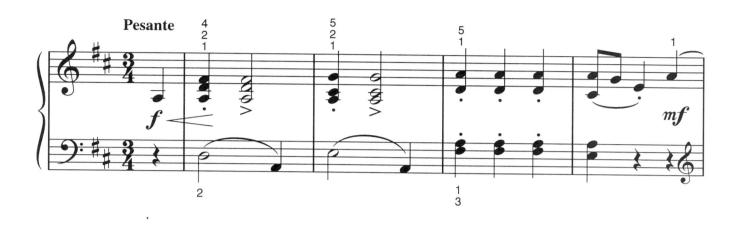

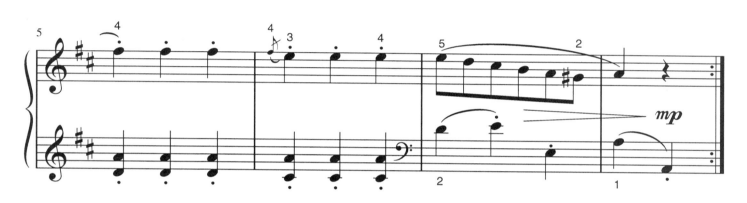

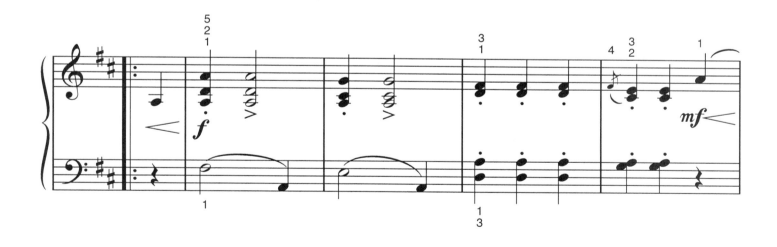

VI.

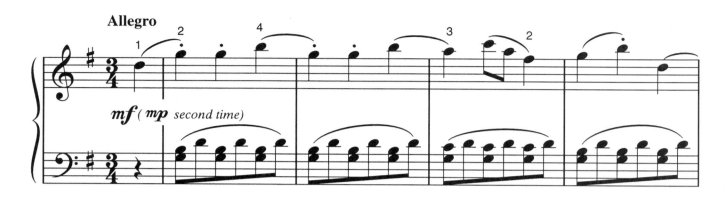

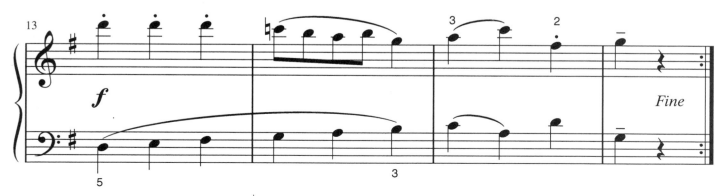

Trio

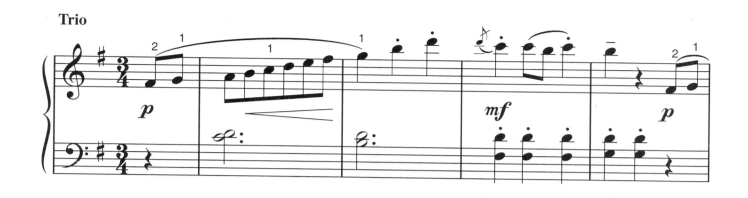

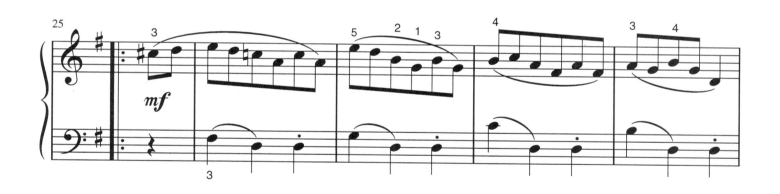

Da capo al fine
2nd time

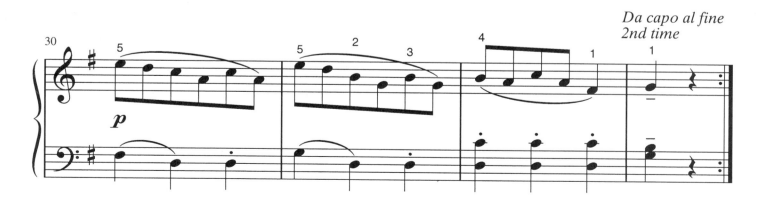

SONATINA

Ludwig van Beethoven

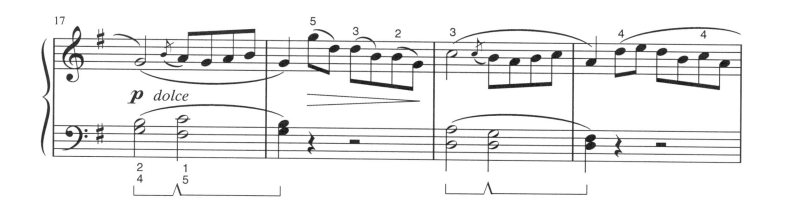

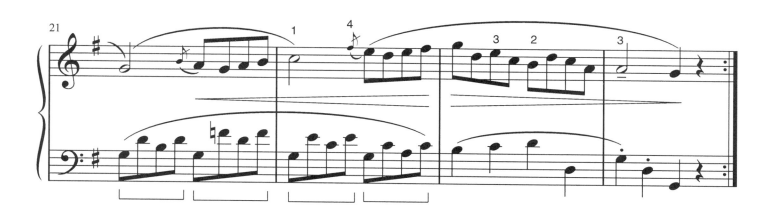

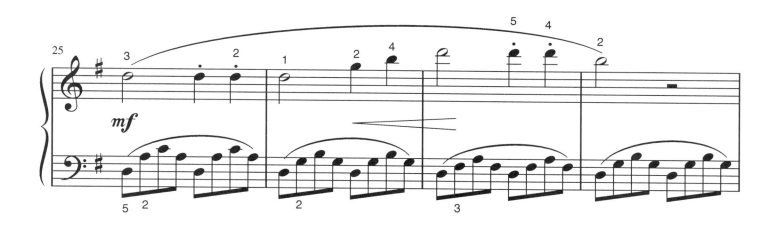

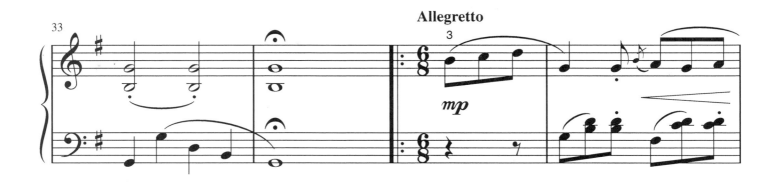

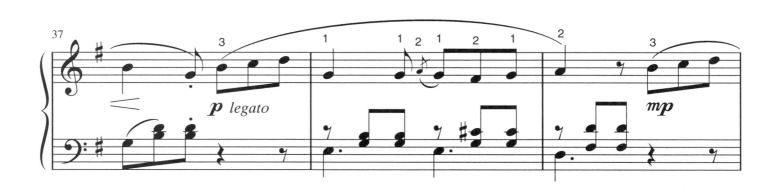

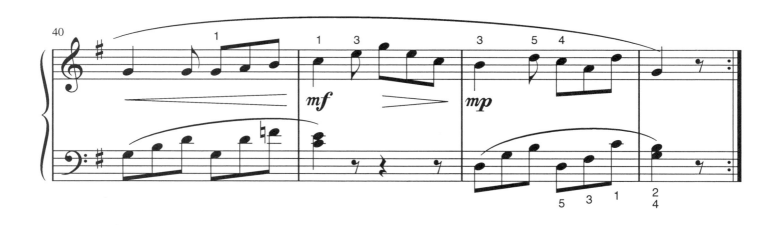

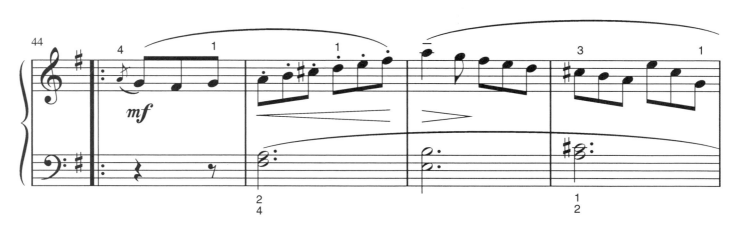

GAVOTTE AND VARIATIONS

Johann Pachelbel

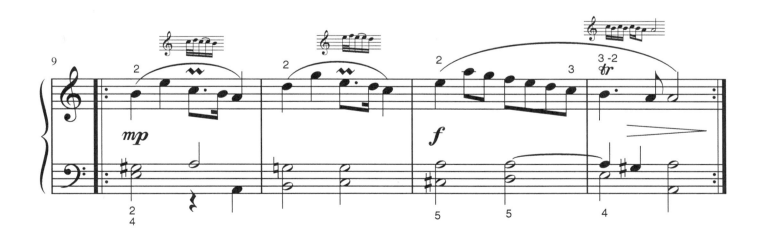

Var. I

Var. II (Sarabande)

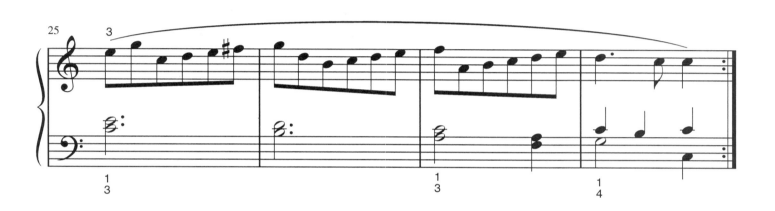

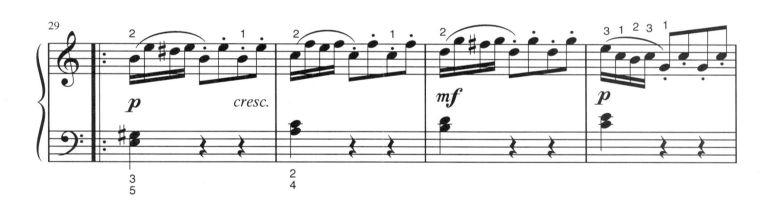

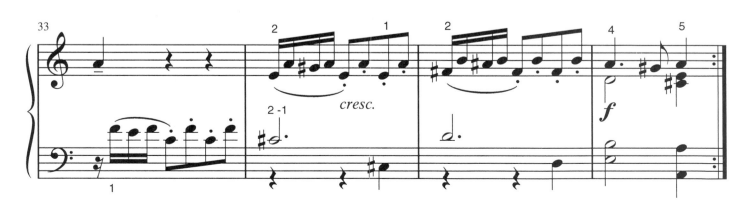

SONATINA

Jakob Schmitt

THE CLOCK

Theodor Kullak

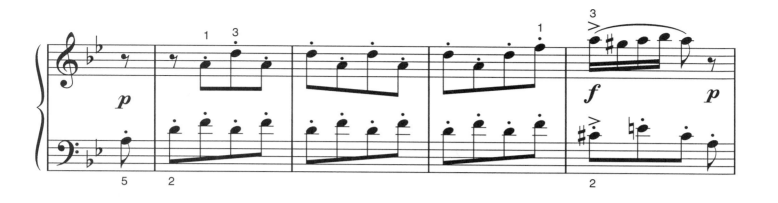

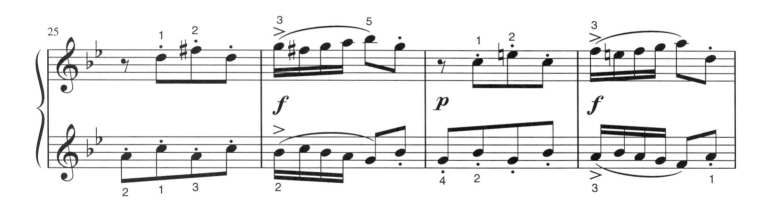

D.S. al Fine

THE WILD HORSEMAN

Robert Schumann

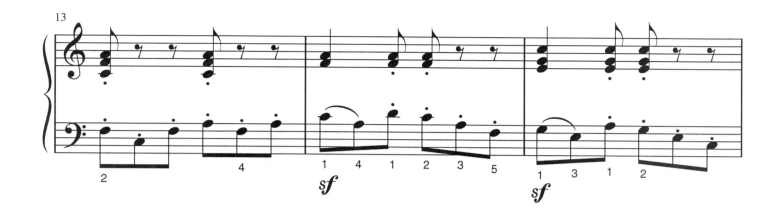

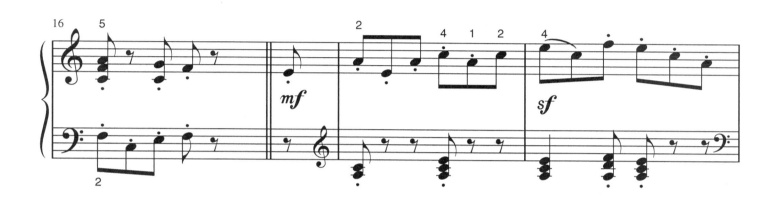

VALSE SENTIMENTALE

Franz Schubert

WALTZ

Franz Schubert

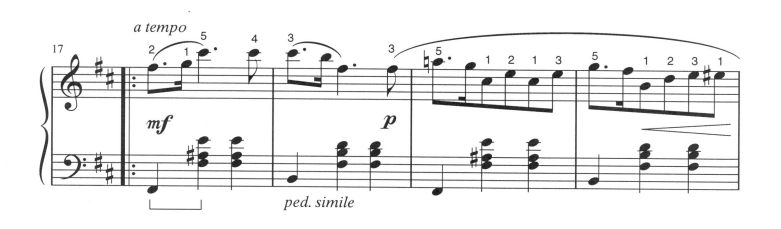

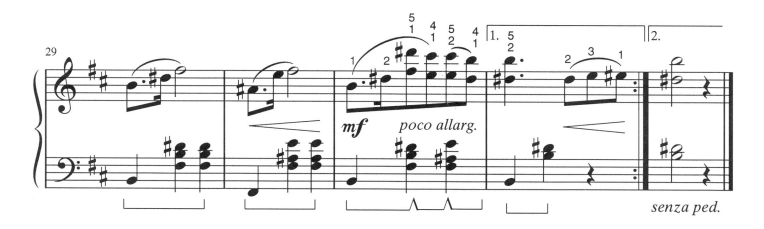

WALTZ

Edvard Grieg

Allegro moderato

(senza pedal)

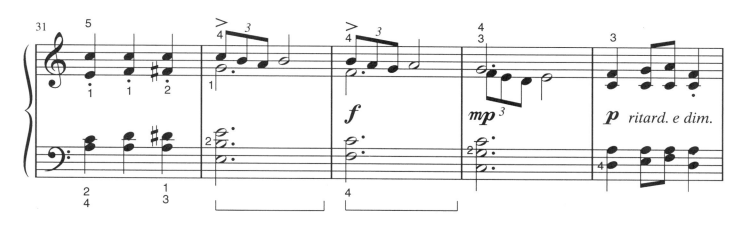

a tempo

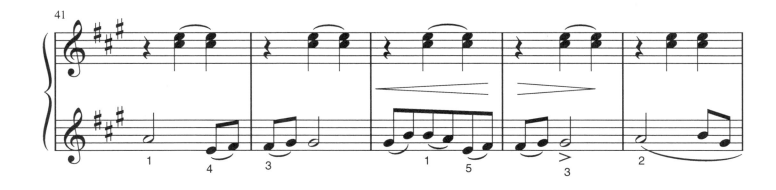

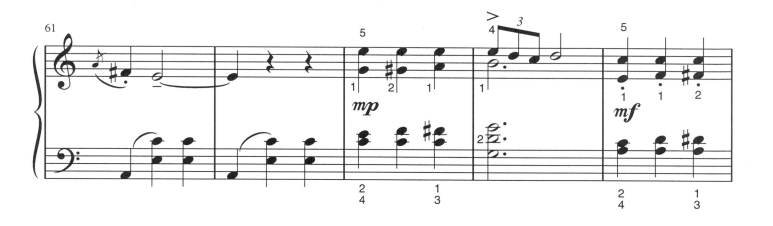

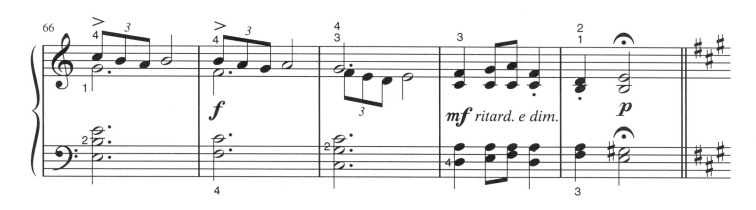

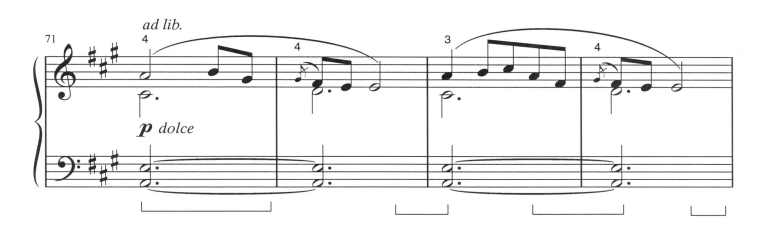

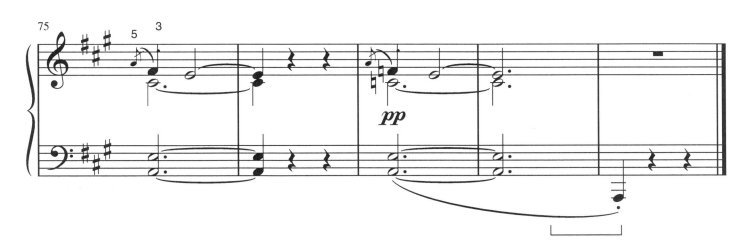

ZINGARESE

Franz Joseph Haydn

*Stem down notes on Fine only

SONATINA

Muzio Clementi

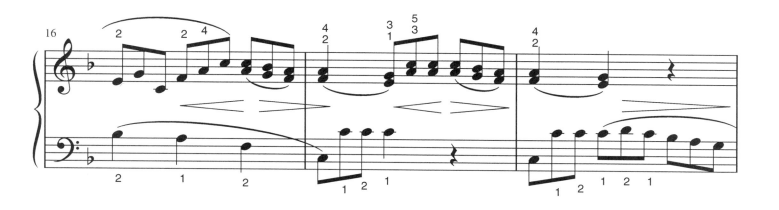

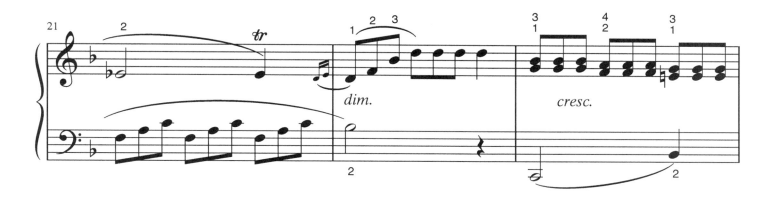

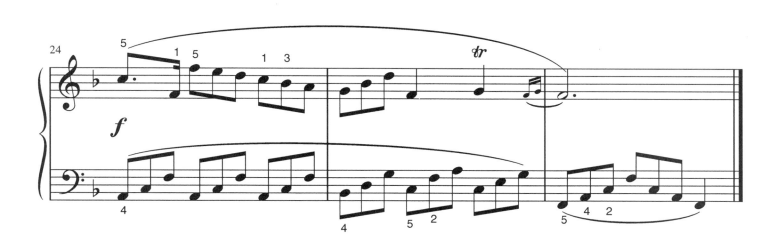